RUSSIAN SACRED MUSIC *for* CHOIRS

*Compiled and edited
by Noëlle Mann*

MUSIC DEPARTMENT

OXFORD
UNIVERSITY PRESS

OXFORD
UNIVERSITY PRESS

Great Clarendon Street, Oxford OX2 6DP,
United Kingdom

Oxford University Press is a department of the University of Oxford.
It furthers the University's aim of excellence in research, scholarship,
and education by publishing worldwide. Oxford is a registered trade mark of
Oxford University Press in the UK and in certain other countries

ISBN 978-0-19-343687-9

Music and text origination by Katie Johnston

Printed in Great Britain on acid-free paper by
Halstan & Co. Ltd, Amersham, Bucks.

PREFACE

This anthology has been conceived to open up some of the wonderful repertoire of Russian sacred music, which so far has not reached the core choral repertoire outside Russia. To this day the greater part of this repertoire is available in Church Slavonic only, the arcane language of the Russian Orthodox Church, and few choir masters are familiar with Eastern Orthodoxy, its music and rituals, its composers, or indeed with the performance style of the Orthodox repertoire. Consequently, selecting works for performance can be a bewildering and intimidating experience to the non-specialist choral director who possesses neither the language nor the basic liturgical knowledge to perform this repertoire without guidance. The anthology addresses these issues in a number of ways:

- It introduces composers who, although central to musical developments in Russian sacred music, have remained little- or un-known outside Russia. Each composer is introduced within his historical context.

- It makes available a system of pronunciation that should provide non-Russian-speaking choir directors and singers with a degree of confidence, allowing them to concentrate on the musical aspect of performance.

- It provides an English translation for every piece so that choirs are able to understand the meaning of the text.

- The majority of the works in the anthology can be performed either in concert or during Church services. In the introductory notes, each work is placed within its liturgical context.

This anthology does not aspire to give a full account of all the styles that evolved throughout the centuries—it is not an academic historical anthology but a singing tool for choirs who seek a new, inspiring repertoire. It nevertheless covers a wide-ranging repertoire spanning from the eighteenth century to the twentieth century. All pieces are for mixed chorus, with the exception of the monodic chants in the appendix, which should be performed in unison. There is also one alternative version for male voices only.

Most of the repertoire is liturgical. Orthodox liturgical music comprises broadly two categories: a wide range of hymns and prayers traditionally sung by the choir; and acclamations and dialogues exchanged between the choir and deacon or congregation. This anthology concentrates on the most common hymns and prayers of the Divine Liturgy and the All-night Vigil, but also includes a few non-liturgical pieces that are particularly appropriate for concert performance. While I have included at least one example of some of the prayers that correspond to the musical parts of Western Christian services, such as the Lord's Prayer, Hail Mary, and Gloria, I have endeavoured to illustrate the amazing range and beauty of the texts sung during Orthodox services, with musical settings that belong to different historical periods. Some texts, such as the Lord's Prayer, the Cherubic Hymn from the Liturgy, and 'Gentle Light' from the Vigil, have been set over the centuries by a great many composers, priests, and monks. They are therefore given a predominant place in this collection.

Some eminent composers who contributed to this repertoire—such as Mikhail Glinka, Nikolai Rimsky-Korsakov, and Mily Balakirev—have been omitted to the benefit of less well-known composers, namely Alexander Kastalsky, Pavel Chesnokov, and Alexander Grechaninov, who proved to be more innovative, prolific, and influential than their famous counterparts. Over years of practice as a choir director, I have come to recognise the immense craftsmanship and originality of these three composers, and consequently their works make up the core of this collection. In the case of the two towering masters, Tchaikovsky and Rakhmaninov, I have avoided their most famous works such as their Divine Liturgy and All-night Vigil, which are widely available in the West, in favour of lesser-known pieces, two of which stand out as representative of their unique style.

Finally, a word about the post-revolution twentieth century. After the watershed of 1917, most churches and monasteries were either destroyed or taken over as military storehouses. Religious services all but disappeared and sacred music was no more heard in concert, especially under Stalin. Like so many artistic endeavours in Soviet Russia, sacred music went underground or moved abroad with the exiled Church, mainly to France and the USA. In Russia, where religious centres were fast vanishing, church composers disappeared, and the few secular composers who secretly approached sacred music, such as Georgy Sviridov, did so as a private response to the absence of spirituality that characterized Soviet life. Consequently, their style followed a new path and reflected the developments that were taking place in secular music, rather than those in Orthodox life.

NOËLLE MANN

About the Editor

Noëlle Mann was born in 1946 in south-west France. Having trained first as a concert pianist, she moved to the UK and read music at Goldsmiths College (University of London), where she began researching the *znamenny* chant of the Russian Orthodox Church. Noëlle's interest in the Russian choral tradition led her in 1993 to establish the Kalina Choir, the first UK choir exclusively dedicated to performing Russian choral music. Through this and subsequent choral directing, she developed her research and performance practice in this area. As a musicologist, Noëlle's interests embraced both Russian choral music and the life and work of Sergei Prokofiev. She became the Founding Curator of the Prokofiev Archive in 1994 and established the academic Centre for Russian Music at Goldsmiths College in 1997. In 2001, Noëlle founded and became Editor of *Three Oranges*, an academic journal dedicated to the study of the life and times of Prokofiev.

Publisher's Note

Noëlle Mann died in 2010, having completed her research, selection, and editing of the pieces in this anthology, but before the work was put into production and published. The publishers are therefore grateful to the following individuals for all their help in this process: Peter Owens, for copyediting the volume and bringing his considerable expertise in the sphere of Russian choral music to the task; Tatiana Soloviova, for creating the substantial preliminary material based on Noëlle's notes and her own research; and Evgeny Tugarinov, for lending his voice to create an accurate audio pronunciation guide.

Before her death, Noëlle tasked Julia and Kristian Hibberd, her daughter and son-in-law, with the completion of the anthology. Kristian, in particular, has contributed to all aspects of the production. The publishers, as well as other members of Noëlle's close family, are especially grateful for their wholehearted support of the project and for ensuring that Noëlle's vision was honoured.

The published collection serves as a fitting tribute to Noëlle's expertise, passion, and dedication, and reflects a lifetime's work on this important and largely unexplored catalogue of works.

CONTENTS

INTRODUCTION

RUSSIAN SACRED MUSIC: FROM OBLIVION TO THE FOREFRONT OF CULTURAL LIFE

'No one who has ever heard Russian church music properly rendered can refrain from an expression of admiration and exaltation', wrote the American musician Lindsay Norden following a visit to Russia at the beginning of the twentieth century.[1] This collection, while covering a period from the eighteenth to the twentieth century, pays particular attention to music written at that very time—described by musicologists as a 'Golden Age' of Russian sacred music—by such composers as Alexander Kastalsky, Alexander Grechaninov, and Pavel Chesnokov. If during previous epochs church music was a marginalized area confined mostly to services, with little relevance to the mainstream of Russian culture, from 1890 to 1917 it was becoming a major cultural phenomenon admired by Russians and foreigners alike.

When describing their work, Kastalsky, Grechaninov, and Chesnokov used the terms 'New Direction' and the 'Moscow School', since this renaissance of church music was centred on the Moscow Synodal School—the leading educational institution for liturgical music, with which all three composers were closely connected. Formulating the goals of the New Direction, they stated that sacred compositions should be based on authentic traditional chants, be national in spirit, and be a true church music, 'as distinct from secular music as the church vestments are from the dress of the laity'.[2] Their compositions resurrected that which had been forgotten but was not meant to die: ancient Russian sacred chants.

After conversion to Christianity in AD 988, Russia was for some time under the influence of Byzantine music. However, highly original traditional chants, such as *znamenny*, *putevoy*, and *demestvenny*, were soon developed. The origins of these chants are yet to be fully explored, but it is beyond doubt that they comprise a *corpus melodiarum* 'unlike anything else whether in the Middle Ages or in more modern times'.[3]

Early harmonization and Western domination

The first Western-style harmonizations of these chants appeared in the seventeenth century, and were mostly influenced by contemporary Polish and Ukrainian music. This development was connected with political changes at the time, when Russia was progressively opening itself to other nations, as well as with the reforms inside the church under the Patriarch Nikon. Following the radical changes of Peter the Great in the early eighteenth century, enforced westernization of Russian life, and increased foreign influence among the Russian upper classes, traditional liturgical singing began to be suppressed by new compositions in a free style, with no connection to the old chants. The chants soon became the preserve of provincial monasteries, villages, and poor towns that could not afford a trained choir to sing music in the fashionable Italian style. This estrangement of church music from its proper source is considered one of the great and tragic enigmas of Russian musical history.

During the eighteenth century, the Imperial Chapel in St Petersburg, the new capital, became the centre of excellence for church singing and officially sanctioned the style of music to be sung throughout the immense Russian Empire. Italian composers Francesco Araja, Baldassare Galuppi, Giuseppe Sarti, and others were invited to teach in Russia. The successive styles established by the Imperial Chapel subsequently moved from the Italian flourish of the sacred concerto (*dukhovny contsert*) under Dmitry Bortniansky to the more homophonic textures of German hymnography under Alexei Lvov. Dazzling examples of

Russian musical classicism are exhibited in this anthology in works by Maxim Berezovsky ('Do Not Reject Me in My Old Age', No. 7) and Artem Vedel ('Blessed is the Man', No. 4). Works such as these are expressive, emotional, and masterly in their use of vocal resources, yet they had little in common with Russia's native liturgical singing. After nearly two hundred years of dominating foreign influence, Russian sacred music had not only nearly lost its character, it did not correspond with the spirit of the Orthodox Church: 'I appreciate certain merits in Bortniansky, Berezovsky, and others; but how little their music is in keeping with the Byzantine architecture, the ikons, and the whole spirit of the Orthodox Liturgy!', wrote Tchaikovsky in 1878.[4]

In 1772, the Holy Synod (the governing body of the Russian Church) published a collection of traditional chants that made up the most common services of the Orthodox Church. This unprecedented publication was a Russian protest aiming to save the national heritage at the time when music was totally subjugated to foreign styles. In the nineteenth century, medieval scholars such as Vladimir Odoevsky, Dmitry Razumovsky, and Stepan Smolensky carried out extensive research on the ancient chants and their unique neumatic notation. They laboured continuously to familiarize the Russian public with their musical heritage, which was eventually followed by a phenomenal rise in interest in the traditional chants.

The principles of the New Direction

The most important and controversial issue in the reintroduction of traditional chants (with their free asymmetrical rhythms and austere diatonic tunes) was the question of their harmonization, which for many years could not be satisfactorily resolved.[5] Kastalsky commented: 'Our original church tunes when laid out chorally lose all their individuality; what distinction they have when sung in unison as they were by the old-believers, and how insipid they are in the conventional four-part arrangements of our classics'.[6]

The composers and theorists of the New Direction found the way forward in the development of the theory of 'national counterpoint', which meant harmonizing the chants using *podgolosok* polyphony (*podgolosochnaya polifoniya*), as typically exhibited in Russian, Ukrainian, and Belorussian folk singing. The musical fabric is formed from the fundamental voice, accompanied by 'under-voicelets' (translated from *podgolosok*), which are themselves variants of the basic melody. Characteristic features include the use of dissonance (within a consonant framework), crossing parts, and the simultaneous pronunciation of syllables. One of the many examples of *podgolosok* polyphony in this anthology can be found in Kastalsky's 'A Mercy of Peace' (No. 1).

Among the most successful representatives of the New Direction were Kastalsky, Grechaninov, Chesnokov, Rakhmaninov, Kalinnikov, and Smolensky. Despite some diversity—Kastalsky generally avoided changing the chants (see Nos. 1, 6, and 27), while Grechaninov was freer, composing in the style of Russian antiquity (see Nos. 2 and 21)—the movement had its definite character. Smolensky (Director of the Moscow Synodal School) and Professor Antonin Preobrazhensky—the main ideologists of the New Direction—summed up their guiding principles:

- The use of ancient sacred chants, so that 'in new compositions the chants kept their life, flexibility, the mighty force of their expressiveness and beauty'. The chants were not just *cantus firmi* for harmony, as in harmonizations of the early nineteenth century: 'they began to be the main criteria of the style, they dictated the style'.

- The creation of new melodies using typical melodic and rhythmic formulae of ancient chants, thus 'combining the historic approach, national heritage, and free creativity'.

- Developing 'national counterpoint' and arranging sacred chants in the style of folk songs: 'we can consider Russian only those elements that have crystallized in Russian folk music'.[7]

Alongside the unprecedented flowering in the number of compositions, this renaissance of sacred music in Russia included several other simultaneous developments, among which were:

- the opening of a 'History of Church Singing' department at the Moscow Conservatoire in 1867, and later at St Petersburg University, thus establishing church music on a par with secular music;

- growing attention and debate regarding spirituality and nationality of sacred music among the general public in leading newspapers;[8]

- the new and unusual practice of performing sacred music in concert halls, beginning around 1865, which included many triumphant visits of Russian choirs abroad.

The nationalist resurgence

The New Direction certainly established a national style in sacred music, and this should be viewed within the context of the national revival in the other arts around the same time.[9] While composers were reviving ancient chants, archaeologists and painters were restoring old icons, cleaning the 'black boards' of centuries of dirt and later additions to reveal the bright colours and amazing expressiveness of ancient art. In 1903, for example, Vasily Guryanov and his team discovered the now famous fifteenth-century 'Trinity' icon by Andrei Rublyov.

In a broader context, the renaissance of Russian sacred music and the neo-Russian style in art can be compared with movements in other European countries, such as:

- the Oxford Movement, which started as a theological development in 1833 in the Anglican Church and had a profound influence on the arts and music in England;

- the ideals of the École Niedermeyer in Paris, formulated around 1853;

- the Caecilian movement in German-speaking Roman Catholicism during the final decades of the nineteenth century.[10]

Sacred music in modern Russia

By the beginning of the twentieth century, sacred music in Russia was no longer the exclusive domain of the church. It had moved to the forefront of cultural life and was seen by many as an important part of the national heritage—the ultimate expression of national consciousness. It became one of the country's chief musical attractions, alongside ballet and opera.

In August 1917, the All-Russian Sobor (the General Council of the Russian Church) was summoned for the first time after the reformation of the church under Peter the Great, and Patriarch Tikhon was elected as the new leader. The Sobor, which concluded in September 1918, paid much attention to the future of church music. However, the October Revolution of 1917 brought with it a fatal break with the past, followed by the most aggressive anti-religious politics, mass destruction of churches, and executions of thousands of believers. Religious rituals and liturgical music were pronounced as relics of the past, incompatible with the new Communist ideology. During the reign of Stalin, any connection with the church meant risking lives and careers.

Khrushchev's 'thaw' in the 1960s had little effect on the oppressive anti-religious politics; indeed, the Communist Party leader promised to show to the world the last priest in Russia. In the late 1970s and 1980s, the situation became a little milder. Though the country still officially confessed atheism, it became acceptable to perform Russian sacred music in concert halls as an example of national heritage. However, the only way to compose sacred music 'legally' and safely was in connection with history. It was in this way that, a few decades earlier, Sergei Prokofiev was able to present his setting of 'Many Years' (Nos. 16 and 17), composed for the film *Ivan the Terrible*, and Georgy Sviridov his *Three Choruses* (including 'Sacred Love', No. 24), for Tolstoy's historic play *Tsar Feodor Ioannovich*.

The perestroika reforms of 1986 and the collapse of the Communist regime in 1991 were followed by a religious renaissance, and the composition and performance of sacred music in Russia is nowadays very prevalent. Several composers, including Anton Viskov (see 'Rejoice, Nicholas, Great Miracle-Worker', No. 22), Metropolitan Hilarion Alfeyev, Sergei Trubachev, Archimandrite Matfei Mormyl, and Vladimir Martynov, have followed in the footsteps of the Moscow School. However, recent research has uncovered further mysteries of Russian liturgical singing, and composers are even better equipped with knowledge of the past. For some of these modern composers, the principles of the New Direction are by no means the only solution to the problem of reconciling ancient monody and harmonization. Others believe that it is impossible to arrange ancient chants without distorting them, and that attempts to reconcile antiquity and modernity are only an illusion.[11]

Notes on the Choral Tradition

Constituency of the choral ensemble

At the beginning of the twentieth century, the art of choral singing was at its peak in Russia. Among the greatest exponents were the choir of the Imperial Chapel and the Moscow Synodal Choir. The Imperial Chapel originated in 1479 in Moscow, though in 1703 it was relocated to the new city of St Petersburg. Initially the choir was made up of men only, but in the seventeenth century, with development of part-singing, boys were also included. Choristers benefitted from a thorough general and musical education alongside their duties in the choir. The Imperial Chapel was the first Russian choir to gain an international reputation, particularly under the directorship of Bortniansky, performing both Russian and European masterpieces. Indeed, in 1824 the choir gave the world premiere of Beethoven's *Missa Solemnis*. The reputation of the Imperial Chapel was such that the Prussian King Frederick William III is said to have used it as a model for his own choir in Berlin. In 1829, the choir was made up of forty men and fifty boys.

The equivalent in Moscow was the Synodal Choir, dating from 1721. Nearly all compositions of the New Direction were given their premiere by the Synodal Choir in the Cathedral of the Dormition of the Mother of God in the Kremlin. By the end of the nineteenth century it was considered to be the best choir in Russia, and consisted of over a hundred boys and men, trained to a high standard. The tours of the Synodal Choir in Europe, starting with their first visit to Vienna in 1899, were always a triumph.

Another remarkable choir of that time in Moscow was the Choral Chapel, under the leadership of conductor and composer Feodor Ivanov, which included two hundred men and boys. In contrast, the hugely popular choir directed by Ivan Yukhov consisted of only thirty singers. To accommodate groups of different sizes, composers occasionally provided two versions of the same piece (Kastalsky's setting of the Great Doxology, No. 27, is one such example; the version included in this anthology is for a larger choir).

In the 1880s, mixed-voice choirs began to appear in Russia, and they quickly established a strong position. In 1905 an experimental 'Symphonic Choir' was formed by Moscow conductor Vyacheslav Bulychev, who wished to explore the expressive effects of mixing different vocal timbres. Bulychev was a long-term friend of Grechaninov, whose concept of 'symphonization of the choir' was certainly influenced by Bulychev's experimentations. In 1925, the choir of the Imperial Chapel, now renamed the State Academic Kapella, was made up of thirty men, twenty-eight women, forty boys, and thirty girls.

Modern performances of Russian sacred music are generally sung by mixed choirs of various sizes. Thus, the Moscow Synodal Choir (disbanded in 1919 and re-established in 2008) now consists of eighty singers, both men and women. There is also an extensive repertoire of arrangements for all-female or all-male ensembles (see Prokofiev's male-voice version of 'Many Years', No. 16).

Challenges for performers

Russian church music presents certain difficulties for both choir directors and singers. Firstly, the greatest challenge of *a cappella* singing is to produce a smooth and well-blended ensemble. Secondly, as this is indeed choral music in the fullest sense of the word, the group of voices should give forth almost as much variety of tone-colour as does the orchestra. Then there is an importance of procuring the line of low basses, which have a particular significance in this type of music. Finally, it is most important to get the style, or rather the spirit, of this music, including the difference between *liturgical* music and *sacred* music. Liturgical music is based on canonical texts and performed as part of a religious service (in the Orthodox Church most services are sung rather than read), while sacred music, music with a spiritual content, is more often than not performed in concert. Sacred music can and often does require personal self-expression, while the sole role of liturgical music is to illumine, to elevate the Word, which must remain at all times clear and understandable to the community. In fact the liturgical singing of the Orthodox Church is a form of worship in itself. This requires a style of performance that tends to negate individual emotion. The choral sound in Orthodox music is merged and rounded, without a hint of solo vibrancy or virtuosity. It is a sound that can be described as 'ascetic'.[12]

The Russian Orthodox repertoire offers many marvellous examples of this ascetic sound, and a large discography is available to explore, including recordings by the State Academic Symphony Capella of Russia, the Russian Patriarch Choir of Moscow, the St Petersburg Chamber Choir, and the male-voice choir Drevnerussky Raspev.

LITURGICAL CONTEXT

The central services of the Orthodox Church

The two most important services of the Russian Orthodox Church are:

- the All-night Vigil, celebrated on Saturday evening (when Sunday begins) and on the eve of the great feasts. The name is reminiscent of the fact that early Christians often celebrated at night, to meet the rising of the sun. In the Russian tradition the Vigil combines the Vespers and the Matins;

- the Divine Liturgy of Saint John Chrysostom, celebrated on Sunday (every Sunday in the Orthodox Church is the day of Resurrection, 'Little Easter') and on weekdays to commemorate certain events in the lives of Christ and the saints.

The layout of an Orthodox church plays an important part in the services. The sanctuary, representing heaven, is separated from the body of the church by a screen (*ikonostasis*), in which there are three doors. In the centre are the Royal Doors, representing the gateway between earth and heaven.

The central hymns of the All-night Vigil

Vespers

'Bless the Lord, O My Soul' (Psalm 104), also known as the opening psalm, symbolizes the creation of the world and is sung in a major key. While it is being sung, the Royal Doors to the altar are opened—a symbol of heaven—and a priest censes the church, which represents the world and humanity. It is a solemn piece reflecting the joyful harmony between the spiritual and physical, Creator and creation. 'Blessed is the Man' (Psalms 1 and 2) is sung after the Royals Doors have been closed; this represents the arrival of evil and sin, and the estrangement of humanity from God. It symbolizes the repentance of Adam and the hope for the salvation of the world through the promised Messiah.

'Gentle Light', one of the earliest Christian texts, is central to the Vespers, and represents the coming of the Saviour promised to the forefathers. The Royal Doors are opened once more, symbolizing that heaven is again open to mankind. A priest comes from the altar, yet through the side door rather than the Royal Doors, representing the coming of Christ not in royal glory but in humility.

The well-known prayer of Simeon from the Gospel of St Luke (Nunc Dimittis) is then performed, followed by the final setting, 'Rejoice, O Virgin Mother of God', which is an important thanksgiving prayer to Mary.

Matins

'Praise the Name of the Lord' (verses from Psalms 135 and 136) is a joyful thanksgiving to God. At this climatic moment churches are brightly lit and incensed to symbolize the Light of Christ that illumines all, and the faithful are annointed with oil. This part is known as *Polyeleos*, meaning 'much oil' or 'much light' in Greek. The Great Doxology is a final song of praise at the end of the Vigil, and is a thanksgiving to God for receiving the gift of Light, both spiritual and material. In the days of early Christianity, the priest's exclamation 'Glory to thee who has shown us the Light' and the Great Doxology would be sung as the sun was rising. This hymn combines the song of the shepherds at the birth of Christ ('Glory be to God on high, and on earth peace'), verses from the Psalms, and the Trisagion prayer (which is also sung at the Liturgy).

The central hymns of the Divine Liturgy

The Liturgy is divided into two parts. The first, called the Liturgy of the Catechumens and open to all, is centred on the mystery of God's Word in sacred scripture, and its central point is the reading of the Gospel. The second, the Liturgy of the Faithful, consists of the Eucharistic offering in the strict sense: thanksgiving, blessing, and consecration of the Holy Gifts, followed by Communion. As the name emphasizes, only confirmed Orthodox Christians may take part in Holy Communion.

The Liturgy of the Catechumens begins with the singing of three antiphons (Psalms 103 and 146, and the Beatitudes), which comprise the preparatory stage. Then the Royal Doors open and the Gospel is brought out from the altar. This is followed by the singing of the Trisagion hymn ('the Angels' prayer'—not to be confused with the Sanctus of the Eucharistic prayer), which is believed to be of heavenly inspiration and was attested for the first time at the Council of Chalcedon in AD 451. With this hymn, Orthodox believers glorify the Holy Trinity. While it is being sung, a priest, on behalf of all, silently prays for the forgiveness of sins. The Trisagion is sometimes preceded by the prayer 'Lord, Save the Faithful' (as in Chesnokov's setting, No. 14), which is a short version of the priest's silent prayer.

The Cherubic Hymn begins the Liturgy of the Faithful. Having 'laid aside all terrestrial cares', believers are preparing to receive the King of All: Christ. The text is based on St John's vision of cherubims worshipping God as described in the book of Revelation.

'A Mercy of Peace' (the Eucharistic prayer—the name refers to the mercy of God, who brings peace to the world through Jesus Christ) is sung straight after a setting of the Credo. It marks the very heart of the mystery that is being celebrated. The beginning is sung as a dialogue between a priest and the choir, which represents the faithful. The choir then chants over the priest as he recites the Eucharistic prayer and invokes the Holy Spirit. Church bells ring at this moment.

'It is Truly Meet'—a hymn in honour of Mary, the Mother of God—is performed next, followed by 'Our Father', the Lord's Prayer, which forms the last stage of the liturgical sequence that leads up to Communion.

'Many Years' is a hymn frequently sung at the end of the Liturgy for a parishioner, lay or clergy, on a day of special celebration in their life—a form of well-wishing in a solemn and festive way. In the Byzantine Empire, it was usually reserved for Emperors, but in Russia it is sung for any Orthodox person, and not necessarily following the Liturgy. It may, for example, be performed after a celebratory meal. For a more authentic performance, 'Many Years' may be preceded by a priest's exclamation (preferably sung by a deep bass voice with gradual rising of pitch and volume): 'Grant unto thy servants, O Lord, a long and peaceful life, health, salvation, and prosperity in all things, and preserve them for many years!' ('Blagodyenstvyennoye i mirnoye zhitiye, zdraviye i spaseniye, i vo vsyem blagoye pospyesheniye podazhd, Gospodi, rabam tvoim i sokhrani ikh na mnogaya lyeta! Благоденственное и мирное житие, здравие и спасение, и во всем благое поспешение подаждь, Господи, рабам твоим и сохрани их на многая лета!') In traditional settings, the choral response would then be repeated three times by the choir.

TATIANA SOLOVIOVA

ENDNOTES

[1]   Norden, N. L., 'A Brief Study of the Russian Liturgy and Its Music', *The Musical Quarterly*, vol. V, no. 3 (1919), p. 450

[2]   Kastalsky, A. D., 'My Musical Career and My Thoughts on Church Music', trans. S.W. Pring, *The Musical Quarterly*, vol. XI, no. 2 (1925), pp. 245

[3]   Swan, A. J., *Russian Music and its sources in chant and folk-song*, London: John Baker (1973), p. 37

[4]   Tchaikovsky, M., *The Life and Letters of Peter Ilich Tchaikovsky*, ed. R. Newmarch, London: John Lane (1905), pp. 298-9

[5]   See Swan, A. J., 'Harmonizations of the Old Russian Chants', *Journal of the American Musicological Society*, vol. II, no. 2 (1949), pp. 83-6

[6]   Kastalsky, Op. cit., p. 238

[7]   Preobrazhensky, A., 'Kul'tovaya musyka v Rossii' [Ritual Music in Russia], *Russkaya dukhovnaya muzyka*, vol. III (1924), pp. 664-7; Smolensky, S., *O blizhaishikh prakticheskikh zadachakh i nauchnykh razyskaniyakh v oblasti russkoi tserkovno-pevcheskoi arkheologii* [On the Immediate Practical Goals and Research Tasks in the Field of Church Singing Archaeology], St Petersburg (1904), pp. 11-12

[8]   This was exemplified by many monographs and articles, including a stream in the newspaper *Moskovskie Vedomosti* between 1899 and 1903, and also through the establishment of such bodies as the *Obshchestvo drevnerusskogo iskusstva* [Society of Ancient Russian Art] in 1864 and the *Obshchestvo lubitelei tserkovnogo peniya* [Society for Lovers of Church Singing] in 1880.

[9]   The birth of the 'New Russian Style' goes back to 1882, when, in Abramtsevo near Moscow, an artistic colony was established to revive Russian folk handicrafts. The colony united painters, sculptors, architects, and musicians, including Viktor Vasnetsov, Mikhail Vrubel, Nicholas Roerich, Alexei Shchusev, and Savva Mamontov. Contemporaries certainly saw the renaissance of sacred music and these movements as united in spirit and, to reinforce this connection, Kastalsky was proclaimed 'Vasnetsov in music' and Rakhmaninov's setting of the All-night Vigil was compared with the rediscovery of ancient icons.

[10]   Campbell, S., Foreword to S. Zvereva, *Alexander Kastalsky: His Life and Music*, trans. S. Campbell, Aldershot: Ashgate (2003), pp. xi-xii. Campbell also compares the developments of the New Direction with the publication of the *English Hymnal* in 1906, 'with its emphasis on plainsong, on the one hand, and folk melodies, on the other, and its compilers' desire to offer an alternative to the worldly values of excessive sentimentality or jovial muscularity found in the music of some Victorian hymns'; and the Schola Cantorum that opened in Paris in 1894, which also expected 'to discover a road to a better future via the past' and 'had a foot in the camp of ethnography'.

[11]   Paisov, Y., 'Besedy s kompozitorami' [Conversations with Composers], *Traditsionnye zhanry russkoi dukhovnoi muzyki i sovremennost*, Moscow: Kompozitor (1999), pp. 229-32

[12]   Gardner, J. von, *Russian Church Singing: Orthodox Worship and Hymnography* (Vol. 1), New York: St Vladimirs Seminary Press (1980), pp. 24-5

EDITORIAL METHOD

The policy throughout the anthology has been to use the best available sources, meaning, predominantly, early printed editions, originating from pre-revolutionary Russia; where possible, these have been first editions, published during their composers' lifetimes (exceptionally, for Prokofiev's settings (Nos. 16 and 17), autograph manuscript material was consulted). The aim has been above all to serve the needs of non-specialist choirs, keeping the music pages as clean and uncluttered as possible. Obvious printing errors have been silently corrected. Beaming, stemming, and syllabic slurs have been made consistent with modern practice. Tempo markings in Italian reproduce those of the sources, except in cases where Russian was preferred: here, a transliteration of the original is placed in parentheses, after an English or Italian translation. Editorial metronome marks, where considered helpful, have been added in square brackets. Dynamics are as found in the sources, although more liberal interventions have been made with respect to the pieces by Vedel and Berezovsky (Nos. 4 and 7) to reflect 18th-century performance practice, which conductors should feel correspondingly free in interpreting. Similar licence may be exercised in the deployment of solo voices, as indicated in the 'choral concertos' by Berezovsky and Rachmaninov (Nos. 7 and 25). The dotted barlines in Chesnokov's 'Blessed is the Man' (No. 3) have been added editorially to serve as structural reference points, though, otherwise, a flowing chant-like rendition would be appropriate (cf. Appendix Ia). Texts from the Divine Liturgy and All-night Vigil are translated by Isabel Hapgood (1851–1928), as is 'The Ever-Vigilant Mother of God' (No. 25), and psalm translations are from the World English Bible, all with some minor alterations.

Psalm numbering in the headings follows Protestant usage. Punctuation, capitalization, and spelling of Cyrillic texts have been modernized according to post-1917 authographical reforms, before transliteration according to the following system:

А а	a		П п	p
Б б	b		Р р	r
В в	v		С с	s
Г г	g		Т т	t
Д д	d		У у	u
Е е	ye; e, following zh, kh, ts, ch, sh, sch		Ф ф	f
			Х х	kh
Ѣ ѣ	(as above)		Ц ц	ts
Ж ж	zh		Ч ч	ch
З з	z		Ш ш	sh
И и	i		Щ щ	sch
Й й	y		Ъ ъ	– (i.e., no symbol)
К к	k		Ы ы	ï
Л л	l		Ь ь	'
М м	m		Ю ю	yu
Н н	n		Я я	ya
О о	o			

The treatment of Аллилуйя is dependent upon its particular musical setting:

    four syllables: al – li – luy – ya
    five syllables: al – li – lu – i – ya

PRONUNCIATION GUIDE

Regardless of the nationality of the composers whose works appear in the anthology, sung texts have been transcribed to reflect a Russian pronunciation of Church Slavonic.

VOWELS

Transcription	Pronunciation
a	as in between bat and jar. Not too open; not too closed.
e	as in fed, net
i	as in meet
o	as in core (deep sound in Church Slavonic)
u	as in boot (deep sound in Church Slavonic)
ï	No English equivalent. To practise this sound, keep the lips spread as in 'ee' and try to say the 'oo' vowel.

NB: all vowels have a single, sustained sound

CONSONANTS

Transcription	Pronunciation
g	as in give: hard 'g' (never as in angel)
zh	as in pleasure
r	as in error and rolled as much as possible
s	as in sit (it should never be pronounced 'z')
kh	as in Scottish loch or German ach
ts	as in Tsar, tsunami
ch	as in check
sh	as in shall
sch	as in fresh, sheep: a slightly longer and harder sound than 'sh'

COMBINATION OF LETTERS

Transcription	Pronunciation
yu	as in you
ya	as in yam
ye	as in yesterday
ey	as in hey
ay	as in buy, but closer to French maille
iy	as in the French fille
oy	as in boy
uy	as in the French nouille
ïy	No English equivalent. See above re 'ï', and follow this with a 'y' sound, as in yet.
an	as in anger (never 'ein' as in angel)

NB: 'oy' must always be pronounced as in 'boy'. Do not confuse with 'oi', which produces two separate vowel sounds (tro-i-tse).

Softening of consonants

The softening, or palatization, of some consonants (indicated by an apostrophe written straight after the consonant) needs to be worked at in singing. It is achieved by placing the tip of the tongue on the ridge of the lower teeth and articulating with the front of the tongue against the hard palate, producing a fleeting 'y' sound *simultaneously* with the preceding consonant (there should only be one sound). Here are some suggestions for the pronunciation of softened consonants:

Transcription	Pronunciation
d'	as in **de**w
n'	as in the French poi**gne**
r'	No English equivalent
s'	as in **s**ee**d**, **s**ew
t'	as in **st**ew
l'	as in **l**eak. It is important to keep this 'clear' sound distinct from the 'dark' variety of 'l', as in the end of lu**ll**.

Letters not included in these tables should be pronounced as their British-English equivalents.

Devoicing of consonants

Voiced consonants (i.e., those accompanied with a vibration of the vocal folds), apart from 'l', 'm', 'n', and 'r', tend to lose their voicing (i) at the end of words, so that:

lyubo**v**	sounds close to	lyubo**f**
mu**zh**	sounds close to	mu**sh**

and (ii) when immediately followed by a voiceless consonant, so that:

vsyekh	sounds close to	**f**syekh
sotvori**v**shemu	sounds close to	sotvori**f**shemu

Guidance from a good model will be helpful in mastering the subtleties of this point.

To download a free audio pronunciation guide to all the texts used in this collection, spoken by Evgeny Tugarinov, visit the *Russian Sacred Music for Choirs* page of **www.oup.com** and click on the link to the Companion Website.

to Nicolas Ossorguine

RUSSIAN SACRED MUSIC
FOR CHOIRS

1. A Mercy of Peace
(*Milost' mira*)

Divine Liturgy

ALEXANDER KASTALSKY
(1856–1926)

The choir responds to the following phrases, sung by the clergy (see p.195 for notes on concert performance)—

① *Deacon:* Stanyem dobrye, stanyem so strakhom: vonmyem, svyatoye voznosheniye v mirye prinositi.

② *Celebrant:* Blagodat' Gospoda nashego Iisusa Khrista, i Lyubï Boga i Ottsa, i prichastiye Svyatago Dukha budi so vsyemi vami.

③ *Celebrant:* Gorye imyeim syerdtsa.

① *Deacon:* Let us stand aright! Let us stand with fear! Let us attend, that we may offer the Holy Oblation in peace.

② *Celebrant:* The grace of our Lord Jesus Christ, and the love of God, and the fellowship of the Holy Spirit be with you all.

③ *Celebrant:* Lift up your hearts.

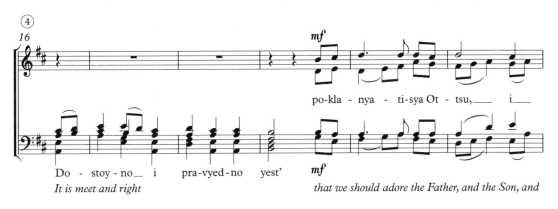

po-kla - nya - ti-sya Ot - tsu, ___ i ___

Do - stoy - no - i pra-vyed - no yest'

It is meet and right ___ *that we should adore the Father, and the Son, and*

Sï - nu, i Svya - to - mu Du - khu, Tro - i - tse Ye - di - no - susch - nyey

the Holy Spirit, ___ *the Trinity, one in essence and undivided.*

i___ Nye-ra - zdyel' - - nyey. ___

rall. (zamedlyaya)

④ *Celebrant*: Blagodarim Gospoda.   ④ *Celebrant*: Let us give thanks unto the Lord.

Svyat,_ Svyat,_ Svyat, Svyat, Go-spod'_ Sa-va-of, is-poln'__ nye-bo i zyem-

Holy, holy, holy, Lord of Sabaoth,   *heaven and earth are full of thy glory.*

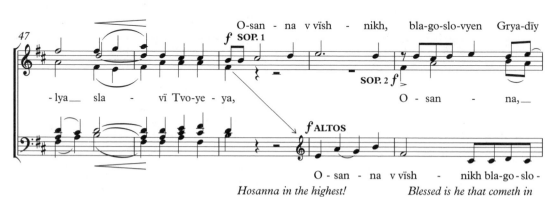

O-san — na v vïsh — nikh, bla-go-slo-vyen Grya-dïy
-lya__ sla — vï Tvo-ye — ya,   O - san — na,__
O - san — na v vïsh — nikh bla-go-slo-

Hosanna in the highest!   *Blessed is he that cometh in*

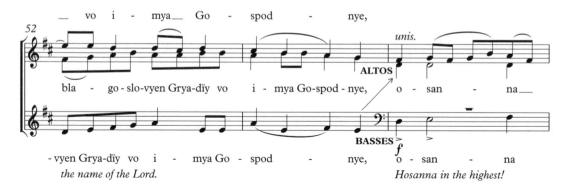

_ vo i - mya__ Go — spod — nye,
bla — go-slo-vyen Grya-dïy vo i — mya Go-spod-nye, o - san — na__
-vyen Grya-dïy vo i — mya Go-spod — nye, o-san — na

the name of the Lord.   *Hosanna in the highest!*

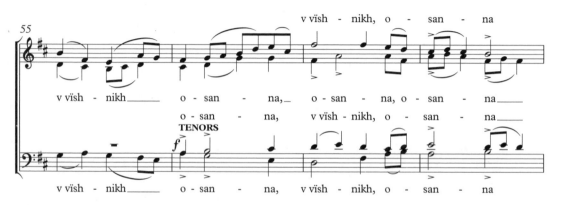

v vïsh — nikh, o — san — na
v vïsh — nikh_____ o - san — na,_ o-san — na, o-san — na_____
o - san — na, v vïsh — nikh, o — san — na_____
v vïsh — nikh_____ o - san — na, v vïsh — nikh, o - san — na

⑤ *Celebrant:* Pobyeduyu pysen' poyusche, vopiyusche, vzïvayusche i glagolyusche:

⑤ *Celebrant:* Singing the triumphant song, crying, calling aloud, and saying:

⑥ *Celebrant*: Priimitye, yaditye, siye yest' Tyelo Moye, yezhe za vï lomimoye vo ostavlyeniye gryekhov.

⑦ *Celebrant*: Piytye ot nyeya vsi, siya yest' Krov' Moya novago zavyeta, yazhe za vï i za mnogi izlivayemaya vo ostavlyeniye gryekhov.

⑧ *Celebrant*: Tvoya ot Tvoikh Tyebye prinosyasche o vsyekh i za vsya.

⑥ *Celebrant*: Take, eat. This is my Body, which is broken for you for the remission of sins.

⑦ *Celebrant*: Drink ye all of this, for this is my Blood of the New Testament, which is shed for you and for many, for the remission of sins.

⑧ *Celebrant*: Thine own of thine own we offer unto thee on behalf of all and for all.

Note: lines 6–8 may be omitted in a concert performance (see p.195)

and we pray unto thee, O our God.

2. Bless the Lord, O My Soul

(Blagoslovi, dushe moya, Gospoda)

All-night Vigil

ALEXANDER GRECHANINOV
(1864–1956)
Op. 59 No. 1

Bless the Lord, O my soul.

Blessed art thou, O Lord.

O Lord, my God,   *thou art become exceedingly glorious.*

Blessed art thou, O Lord.

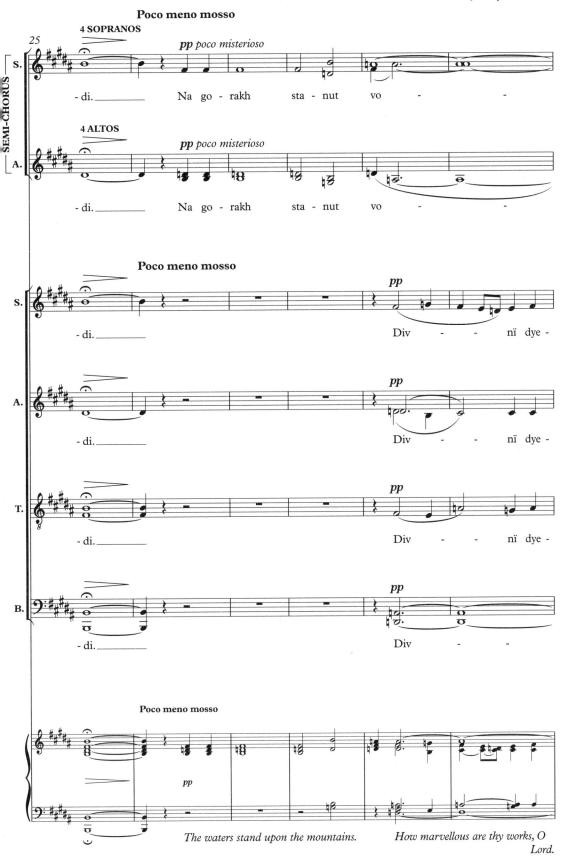

The waters stand upon the mountains.

How marvellous are thy works, O Lord.

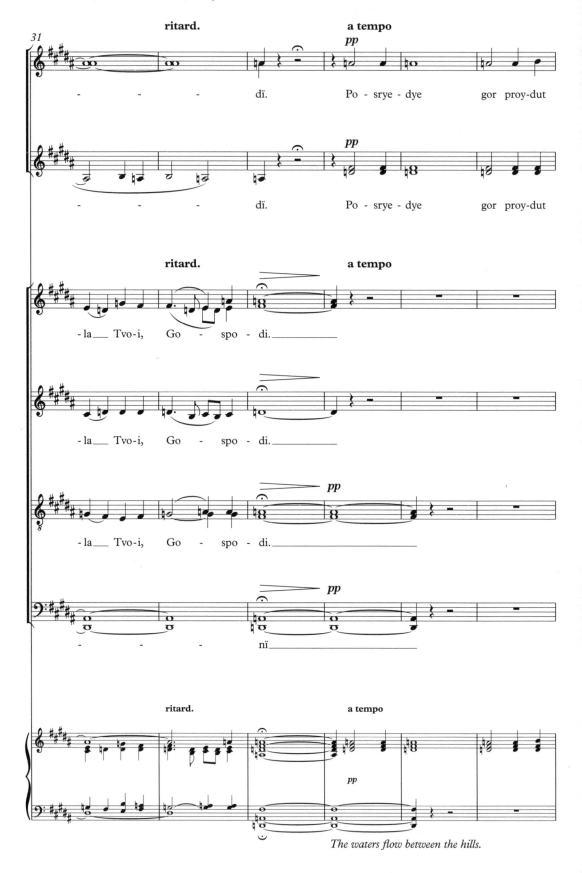

The waters flow between the hills.

*In wisdom hast thou made
all things.*

Glory to thee, O Lord,

who hast created all!   *Glory to the Father, and*

to the Son, and to the Holy Spirit.

Both now and ever, and unto ages of ages.   *Amen.*

Glory to thee, O Lord,

who hast created all!

Glory to thee, O Lord,   who hast created all!

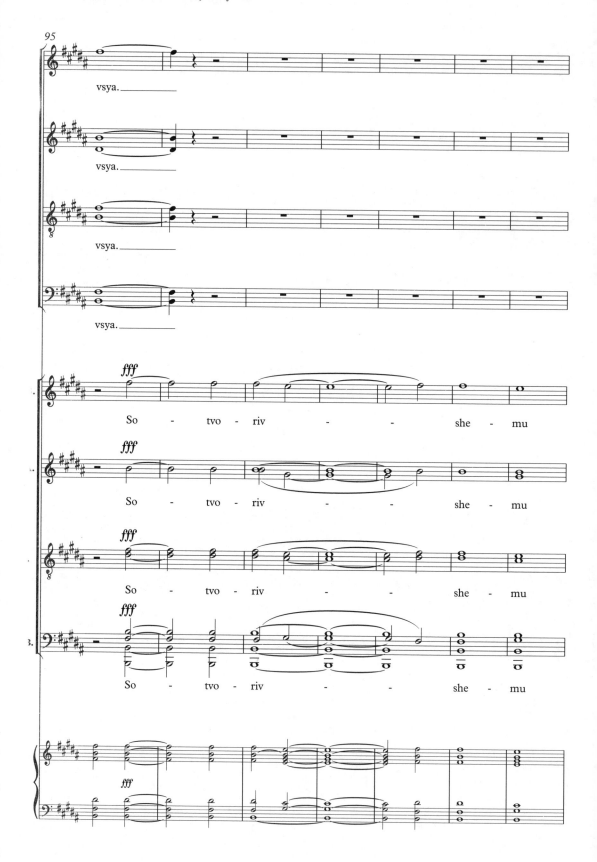

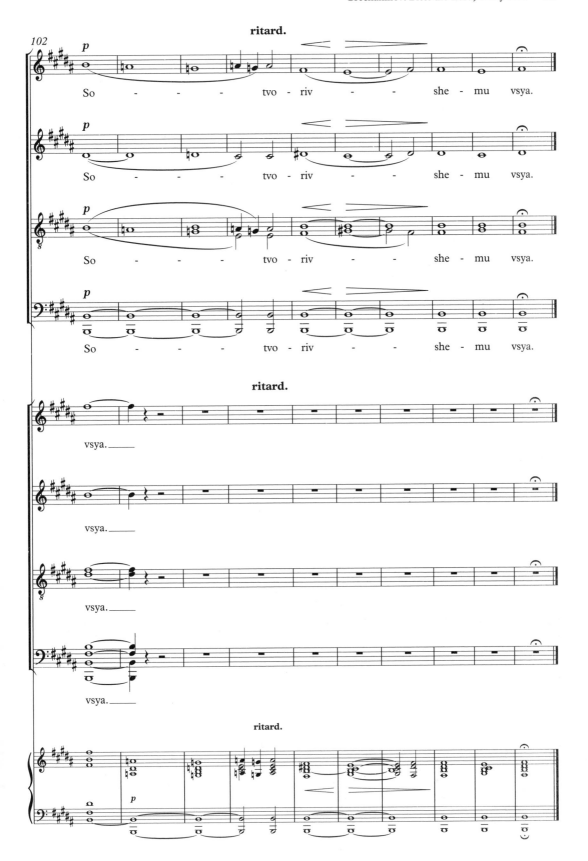

3. Blessed is the Man
(*Blazhen muzh*)

All-night Vigil

PAVEL CHESNOKOV
(1877–1944)
Op. 11 No. 2

of sinners,   *nor sat in the company of scorners.*

Alleluia.

Serve the Lord with fear,

and rejoice unto him with reverence.   *Alleluia.*

Blessed are all they that put their trust in him.

Alleluia.   *Arise, Lord,*   *save me, O my God.*

Salvation is of the Lord,

and thy blessing is upon thy people.

Alleluia.

Glory to the Father, and to the Son, and to the Holy Spirit.

Alleluia.   *Both now and ever, and unto ages of ages.*

                 Amen.   *Alleluia.*

Glory to thee, O Lord.

4. Blessed is the Man

(Blazhen muzh)

All-night Vigil

ARTEM VEDEL
(1767–1808)

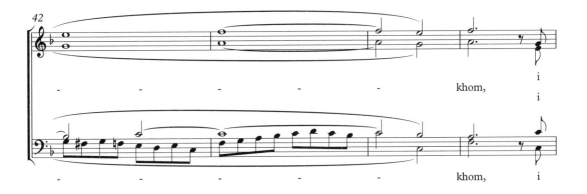

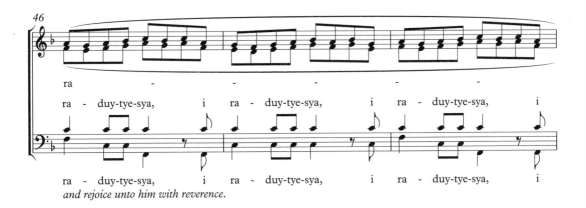

and rejoice unto him with reverence.

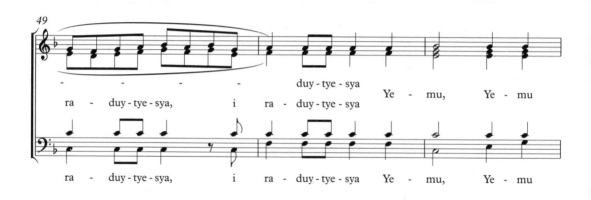

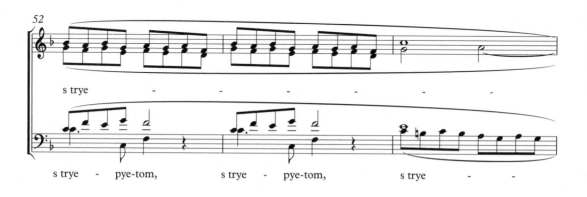

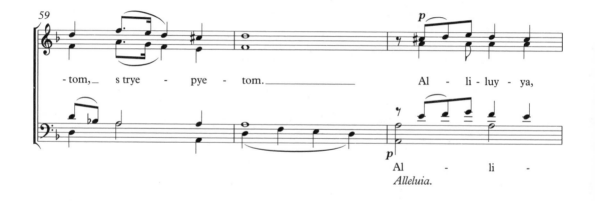

al - li - lu - i - ya.

al - li - luy - ya,   al - li - lu - i - ya.

- luy - ya,   al - li - lu - i - ya.

mf

Bla - zhen - i vsi, na - dye - yu - schi - i - sya nan', bla -

mf

Blessed are all they that put their trust in him.

p

nan'. Al - li - luy - ya,

- zhen - i vsi, na - dye - yu - schi - i - sya

nan'._____

p

nan'.

Alleluia.

f   *p*

al - li - luy - ya,   al - li - lu - i - ya.

f   *p*

Al - li - lu - i - ya.

Salvation is of the Lord,

and thy blessing is on thy people.

Alleluia.

Glory to the Father,   *and to the Son,*

and to the Holy Spirit,

Both now and ever,   *and unto ages of ages.*   *Amen.*

Alleluia.

5. Cherubic Hymn

(Kheruvimskaya pyesn')

Divine Liturgy

PAVEL CHESNOKOV
(1877–1944)
Op. 33 No. 6

Let us, mystically representing the Cherubim,

and intoning the Thrice-Holy chant unto the Life-giving Trinity,

now lay aside all terrestrial cares.

That we may raise on high the King of all,

who is invisibly up-borne by the Angelic Hosts.

Alleluia.

6. Cherubic Hymn

based on the chant 'The Ravaging of Moscow'
(*Kheruvimskaya pysen' 'Na razoryeniye Moskvi'*)

Divine Liturgy

ALEXANDER KASTALSKY
(1856–1926)

tay - no ob - ra - zu - yu - sche, ob - ra - zu - yu-sche, i zhi-vo-tvo -

tay - no ob - ra-zu-yu - sche, i zhi-vo-tvo -

and intoning the

- rya - - - - - schey___ Tro - i -

- rya - - - - - schey___ Tro - i -

Thrice-Holy chant unto the Life-giving Trinity,

-tse tri-svya-tu - yu pyesn', tri-svya-tu - yu pyesn'_____

-tse tri-svya-tu - yu pyesn', tri-svya-tu - yu pyesn'_____

___ pri - pye - va - - yu - sche, tri-svya-tu - yu

___ pri - pye - va - - yu - sche, tri-svya-tu - yu

pyesn'_____ pri - pye - va - - - yu - sche,

pyesn'_____ pri - pye - va - - - yu - sche,

vsya - - - ko - ye, vsya - - ko - ye_____

vsya - - - ko - ye, vsya - - ko - ye_____

now lay aside all terrestrial cares.

nï - nye zhi - tyey - sko - ye,___ nï - nye zhi - tyey - -

zhi - tyey - sko - ye,___ nï - nye zhi - tyey - -

nï - nye zhi - tyey - sko - ye, nï - nye zhi -

- sko - ye___ ot - lo - zhim___ po-pye - che -

- sko - ye___ ot - lo - zhim po-pye - che -

-tyey - sko - ye, zhi - tyey-sko-ye ot - lo - zhim___ po-pye - che -

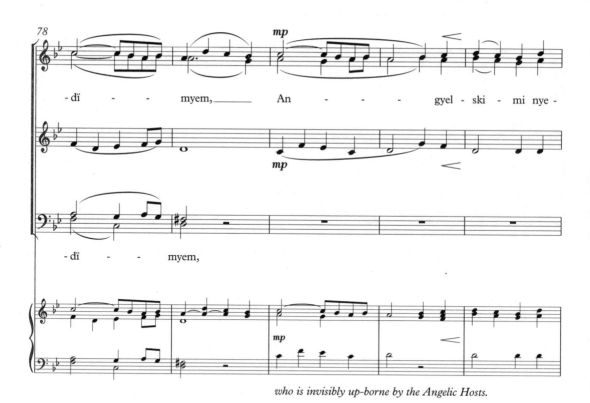

who is invisibly up-borne by the Angelic Hosts.

Alleluia.

7. Do Not Reject Me in My Old Age

(Nye otvyerzhi menye vo vryemya starosti)

Psalm 71: 9–13

MAXIM BEREZOVSKY
(1745–77)

Do not forsake me when my strength fails.

Allegro

-nye. Ya - ko rye - sha vra - zi_____ mo - i mnye, i strye -

For my enemies talk about me,   *and those who*

- gu - - schi - i du - shu mo - yu, i strye - gu - -

i strye - gu - schi - i du - shu mo - yu, i strye -

watch for my soul

- schi - i du - shu mo - yu, i strye - gu - - schi - i

- gu - schi - i du - shu mo - yu, i strye - gu - schi - i

so - vye - scha - sha

du - shu mo - yu, so - vye - scha - sha vku - pye,

du - shu mo - yu,   *conspire together, saying:*

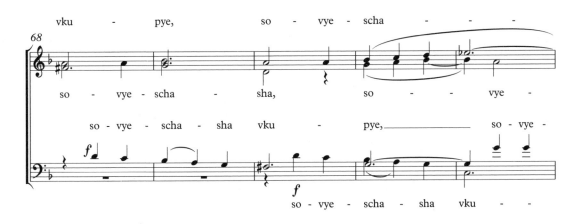

God has forsaken him;

pursue and

take him,   *for no one will rescue him.*

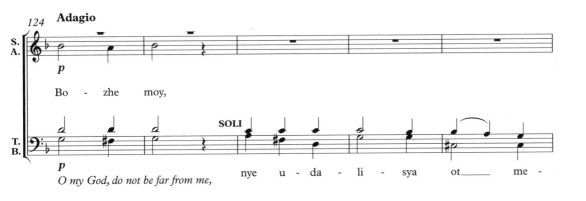

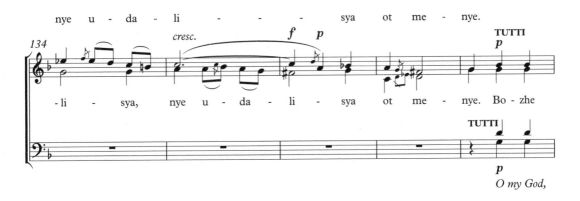

Let my accusers be disappointed and consumed.

(1) Manuscript ADD. 24288 in the British Library includes three E quavers instead of three Fs (a semitone lower). This version of the tenor line is not followed in the extant published editions.

(2) This same manuscript has:

8. Gentle Light

(*Svyetye tikhiy*)

All-night Vigil

ALEXANDER GRECHANINOV
(1864–1956)
Op. 23 No. 2

Gentle light of the holy glory of the Father immortal, heavenly, holy, blessed Jesus Christ!

- stye!_____ Pri - shed - she na___ za - pad soln - tsa,___

In that we now are come unto the setting of the sun,

vi - dyev - she__ svyet vye - cher - niy, po - yem,___ po -

and behold the light of even,

we hymn thee, Father, Son, and Holy Spirit, God.

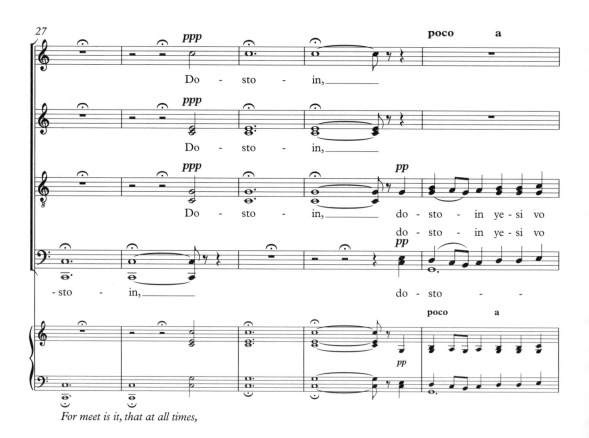

For meet is it, that at all times,

thou shouldest be magnified by voices propitious,

O Son of God, who bestowest life: for which cause all the world doth glorify
thee.

9. Gentle Light

(Svyetye tikhiy No. 3)

All-night Vigil

ALEXANDER KASTALSKY
(1856–1926)

Gentle light of the holy glory of the Father immortal,

heavenly, holy, blessed Jesus Christ!

In that we now are come unto the setting of the sun,

and behold the light of even,

we hymn thee, Father, Son, and Holy Spirit, God.

For meet is it, that at all times,

thou shouldest be magnified by voices propitious,

O Son of God, who bestowest life:

for which cause all the world doth glorify thee.

10. I Cry Aloud With My Voice Unto The Lord

(Glasom moim ko Gospodu vozzvakh)

Psalms 142: 1, 2, 6, & 13: 3

ALEXANDER ARKHANGELSKY
(1846–1924)

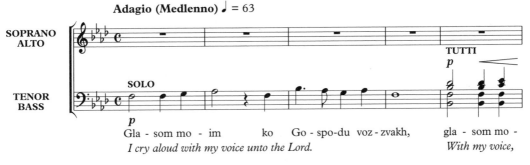

Gla - som mo - im ko Go - spo-du voz - zvakh, gla - som mo -
I cry aloud with my voice unto the Lord.

With my voice,

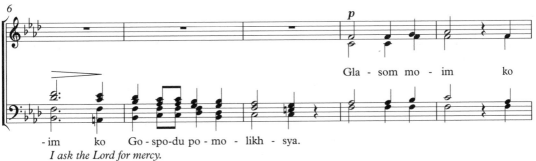

Gla - som mo - im ko

- im ko Go - spo-du po - mo - likh - sya.
I ask the Lord for mercy.

Go - spo-du voz - zvakh, gla - som mo - im ko Go - spo-du po - mo -

- likh - sya.

Gla - som mo - im____ ko Go - spo-du, ko

- likh - sya.____

Gla - som mo - im ko

Go - spo-du voz - zvakh,   gla - som mo - im___ ko _

Go - spo-du po - mo - likh - sya. Pro-li-yu pryed Nim mo - lye - ni -

I pour out my complaints before him.

Pro-li - yu pryed Nim mo - lye - ni - ye   mo - ye,

- ye   mo - ye,___

pro-li-yu pryed

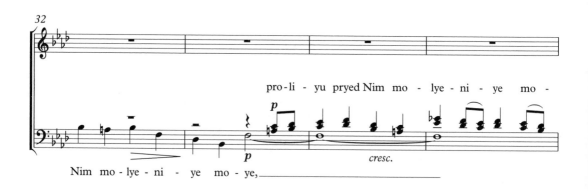

pro-li - yu pryed Nim mo - lye - ni - ye   mo -

Nim mo - lye - ni - ye   mo - ye,___

cresc.

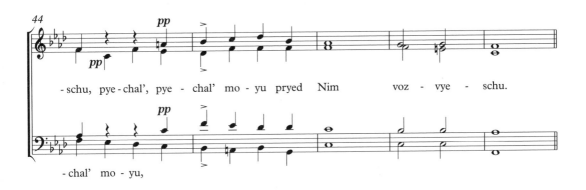

same tempo (v tom zhe tempe)

-ti_____ o - chi mo - i, da nye kog - da u -

to my eyes, lest I sleep in death.

- snu   v smyert'.   Von - mi,   von - mi   mo - lye - ni - yu

Listen to my cry,

a little faster (nemnogo skoree)

mo - ye - mu.   Von - mi,_____ von - mi_____ mo -

p

Von - mi_____   mo ___ ___

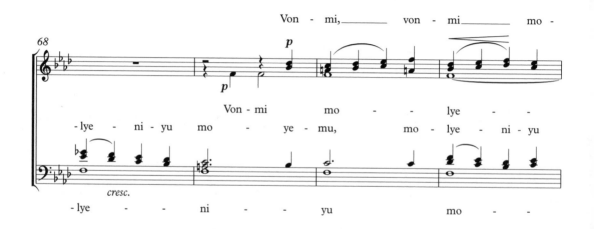

Von - mi,_____ von - mi_____ mo -

Von - mi   mo ___ ___ lye ___ ___

- lye - ni - yu mo - ye - mu,   mo - lye - ni - yu

cresc.

- lye ___ ___ ni ___ - yu   mo ___ ___

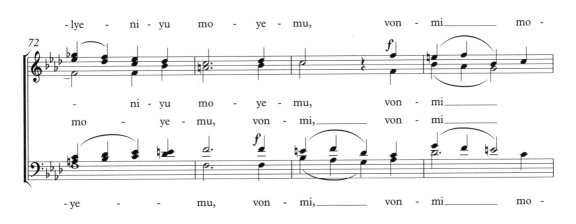

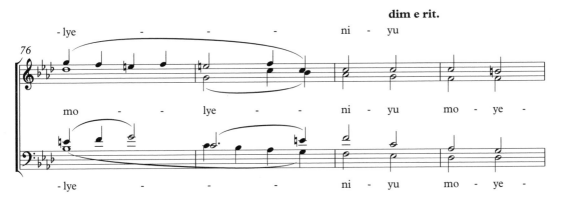

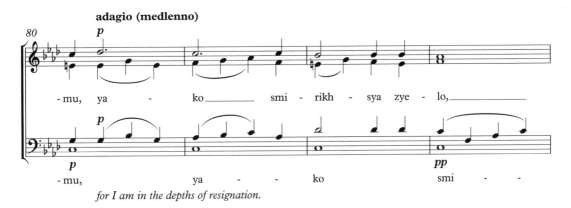

for I am in the depths of resignation.

11. It is Truly Meet

(Dostoyno yest')

Divine Liturgy

Anon. Znamenny chant
harm. N. M. OSSORGUINE and
N. N. KEDROV Jr

Do - stoy - no yest', ya - ko vo - i - sti - nu,

It is truly meet and right

bla - zhi - ti Tya Bo - go - ro - di-tsu, pri - sno-bla-zhen - nu - yu

to bless thee, O Birth-giver of God,   *ever-blessed and pure one,*

i prye-nye-po-roch - nu-yu, i Ma - tyer' Bo - ga na - she-go.

and the Mother of our God.

Chest - nyey - shu - yu khe - ru - vim,_____ i slav - nyey-shu - yu

More honourable than the Cherubim *and beyond compare more glorious*

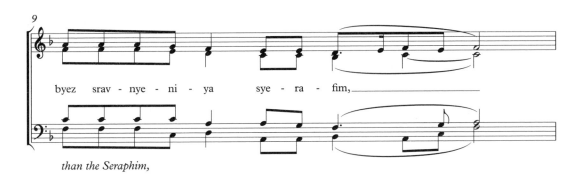

byez srav - nye - ni - ya sye - ra - fim,_____

than the Seraphim,

byez is - tlye - ni - ya Bo - ga Slo - va rozhd - shu - yu,

thou who without corruption barest God the Word;

su - schu - yu Bo - go - ro - di-tsu, Tya___ vye - li - cha-yem, vye - li - cha - yem.

true Birth-giver of God, *we magnify thee.*

12. It is Truly Meet
(*Dostoyno yest'*)

Divine Liturgy

ALEXANDER GRECHANINOV
(1864–1956)
Op. 29 No. 10

Allegretto semplice

Do - stoy - no___ yest', ya - ko vo - i -

mf

SOPRANO
ALTO

ya - ko vo - i -

TENOR
BASS

It is truly meet and right

- sti - nu, bla - zhi - - ti Tya

- sti - nu, bla - zhi - ti Tya

Bo -

mf

to bless thee, O Birth-giver of God,

pri - sno - bla -
mf

f

Bo - go - ro - di - tsu,

pri - sno - bla -

mf

pri - sno - bla -

mf

- go - ro - di - tsu,

f

ever-blessed and pure one,

and the Mother of our God.

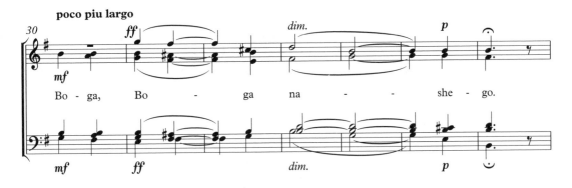

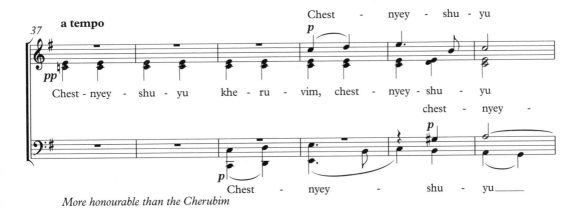

More honourable than the Cherubim

and beyond compare more glorious than the Seraphim,

thou who without corruption barest God the Word;

su - schu - yu Bo - go - ro -

true Birth-giver of God,

rit.   **a tempo**

- - di - tsu, Tya_____ vye - li -

we magnify thee.

(tranquillo)

- cha - - - - - - yem,

meno mosso

vye - - li - cha - - - yem.

13. Let My Prayer Arise

(Da ispravitsya molitva moya)

Psalm 141: 2, 1, 3, 4

PYOTR TCHAIKOVSKY
(1840–93)

like the evening sacrifice.

CHORUS after each verse

Lively (Ozhivlenno) [♩ = 108]

Let my prayer arise before thee like incense,

and the lifting up of my hands like the evening sacrifice.

VERSE 2
Slow

Go - spo-di, voz - zvakh, _____ voz-zvakh k tye-bye, _____ u - slï - shi

Go - spo-di, voz-zvakh _____ k tye - bye, _____

Go - spo - di, voz-zvakh, voz-zvakh k tye-bye, _____ u - slï - shi, u -

Lord, I have cried to thee, hear me;

mya,   u - slï - shi_ mya: _____   von - mi,   von - mi _____

u - slï - shi mya, u - slï - shi mya: von - mi _____ gla-su,   von -

- slï - shi mya, u - slï - shi_ mya: _____   von - mi,   von -

listen to my voice when I call to thee.

CHORUS

gla - su mo - lye - ni - ya mo - ye - go.

- mi gla - su mo - lye - ni - ya mo - ye - go.

- mi gla - su mo - lye - ni - ya mo - ye - go.

VERSE 3
Slow
SOLO

Po - lo - zhi,_____ Go - spo - di,_____ khra - nye - ni -

Po - lo - zhi, Go - spo - di,_____

Po - lo - zhi,_____ Go - spo - di,_____ khra - nye - ni -

Keep watch, O Lord, before my mouth;

keep the door of my lips.

CHORUS

VERSE 4

Do not incline my heart to evil;

make no excuses for my sins.

14. 'Lord, Save the Faithful' and Trisagion

('*Gospodi, spasi*' i *Trisvyatoye*)

Divine Liturgy

PAVEL CHESNOKOV
(1877–1944)
Op. 38, No. 1

* Chesnokov noted: this work should be performed in a light, calm, prayerful, and happy spirit.

© Oxford University Press 2013. Photocopying this copyright material is ILLEGAL.

Kryep - kiy,___ Svya - tïy Byez - smyert - nïy, po - mi - luy
Kryep - kiy, Svya - tïy___ Byez - smyert - nïy, po - mi - luy

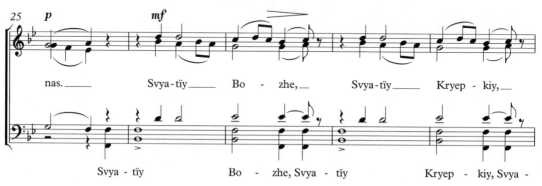

nas.___ Svya - tïy___ Bo - zhe,___ Svya - tïy___ Kryep - kiy,___
Svya - tïy Bo - zhe, Svya - tïy Kryep - kiy, Svya -

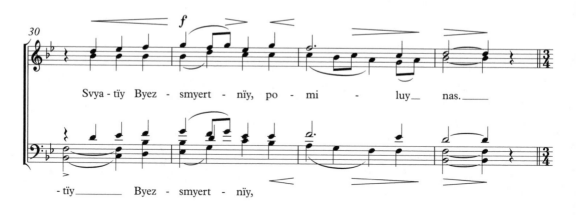

Svya - tïy Byez - smyert - nïy, po - mi - luy___ nas.___
- tïy___ Byez - smyert - nïy,

Sla - va Ot - tsu, i Sï - nu, i Svya - to - mu Du - khu, i nï - nye i pri - sno i vo

Glory to the Father, and to the Son, and to the Holy Spirit,   both now and ever, and unto ages of ages.

15. Many Years
(*Mnogaya lyeta*)

Traditional acclamation

DMITRY BORTNIANSKY
(1751–1825)

[May the Lord grant] many years!

16. Many Years
(*Mnogaya lyeta*)

Traditional acclamation

SERGEI PROKOFIEV
(1891–1953)

Mno - ga - ya lye - ta, mno - ga - ya lye - ta, mno - ga - ya, mno - ga - ya,

[May the Lord grant] many years!

mno - ga - ya lye - ta! Mno - ga - ya lye - ta, mno - ga - ya lye - ta,

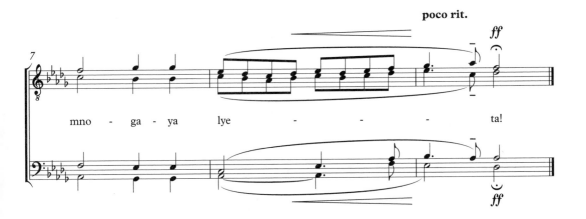

mno - ga - ya lye - - - ta!

17. Many Years

(Mnogaya lyeta)

Traditional acclamation

SERGEI PROKOFIEV
(1891–1953)

[May the Lord grant] many years!

18. Our Father
(*Otche nash*)

Divine Liturgy

NIKOLAI GOLOVANOV
(1891–1953)
Op. 9, No. 3

on earth as it is in heaven.

Give us this day our daily bread,   *and forgive us our trespasses,*

as we forgive those who trespass against us;

and lead us not

into temptation,

but deliver us from evil.

19. Our Father

(*Otche nash*)

Divine Liturgy

ALEXANDER GRECHANINOV
(1864–1956)
Op. 29, No. 11

thy will be done,

Give us this day our daily bread,   *and forgive us our trespasses,*

as we forgive those who trespass against us;

and lead us not into temptation,

but deliver us from evil.

20. Our Father
(*Otche nash*)

Divine Liturgy

ALFRED SCHNITTKE
(1934–98)

No. 3 from *Three Sacred Songs* © 1984 by permission of Musikverlag Haus Sikorski GmbH & Co. KG, Hamburg. Used by permission.

Give us this day our daily bread,

and forgive us our trespasses,

as we forgive those who trespass against us;

and lead us not into temptation,

but deliver us from evil;

for thine is the Kingdom,

the power, and the glory for ever.　　　　　*Amen.*

21. Praise the Name of the Lord

(*Khvalitye imya Gospodnye*)

All-night Vigil

ALEXANDER GRECHANINOV
(1864–1956)
Op. 59 No. 5

Praised be the Lord out of Zion,

O give thanks unto the Lord,

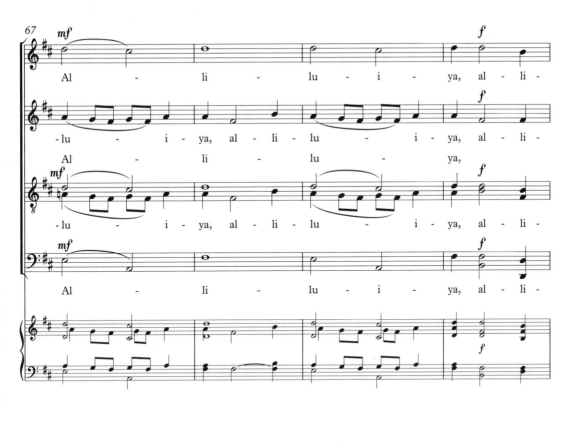

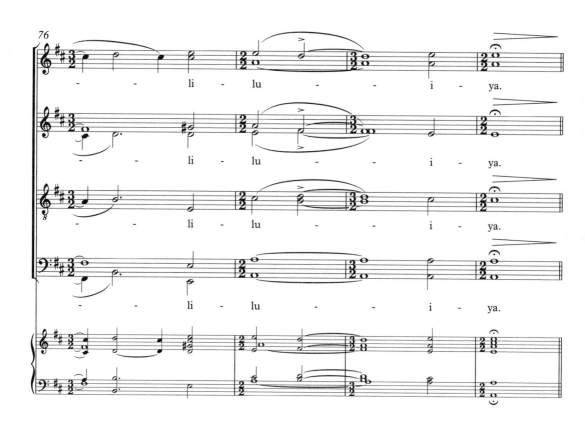

commodo

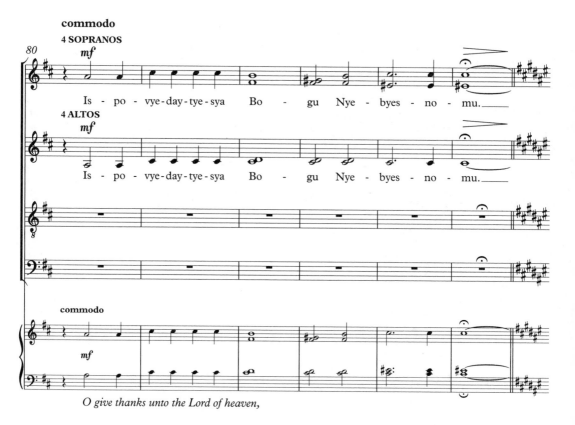

O give thanks unto the Lord of heaven,

for his mercy endureth forever.

Alleluia.

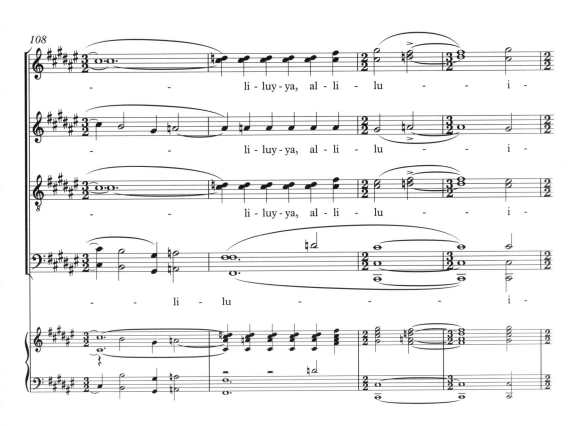

22. Rejoice, Nicholas, Great Miracle-Worker

(Iz Akafista Svyatityelyu Nikolayu)

Akathist to St Nicholas: Kontakion I
trans. Edward Morgan

ANTON VISKOV
(b. 1965)

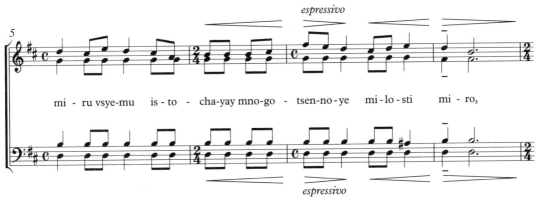

Rejoice, Nicholas, great miracle-worker.

23. Rejoice, O Virgin Mother of God

(*Bogoroditse Dyevo*)

All-night Vigil

VIKTOR KALINNIKOV
(1870–1927)

Rejoice, O Virgin Mother of God!

Mary, full of grace, the Lord is with thee.

Blessed art thou among women,

and blessed is the fruit of thy womb;

for thou hast borne the Saviour of our souls.

24. Sacred Love
(*Lyubov svyataya*)

Alexei Tolstoy
(1817–75)
trans. Edward Morgan

GEORGY SVIRIDOV
(1915–98)

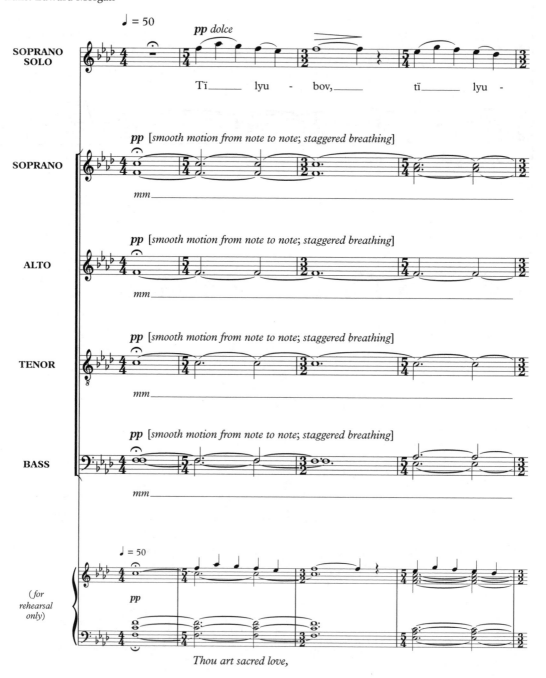

Thou art sacred love,

persecuted from the beginning,   *drenched in blood.*

Thou art sacred love.

25. The Ever-Vigilant Mother of God

(V molitvakh nyeusïpayuschuyu Bogoroditsu)

Kontakion for the Dormition

SERGEI RAKHMANINOV
(1873–1943)

mi - ra_____ nye - prye - lozh - no - ye_____ u - po - va - ni - ye,_____

_____ i_____ v pryed - sta - - - tyel' - stvakh mi - - ra nye-prye -

_____ nye - prye - lozh - no - ye_____ u - po - va - ni - ye,   u - po -

- lozh - - no - ye   u - po - va - - ni - ye,

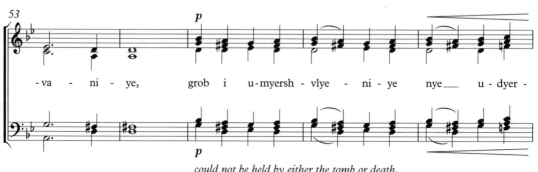

- va - - ni - ye,   grob i u - myersh - vlye - ni - ye   nye_____ u - dyer -

could not be held by either the tomb or death,

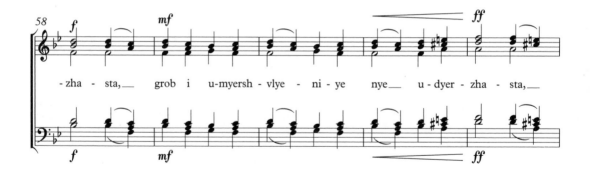

- zha - sta,_____   grob i u - myersh - vlye - ni - ye   nye_____ u - dyer - zha - sta,_____

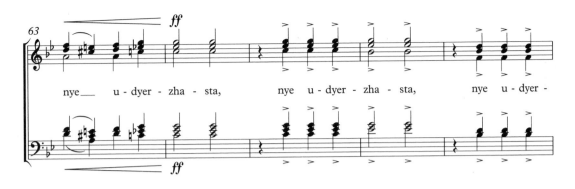

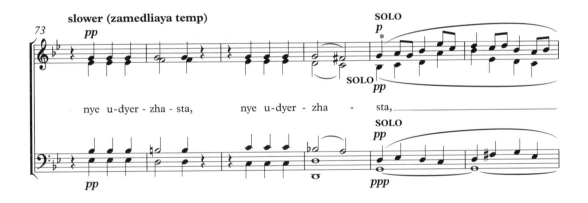

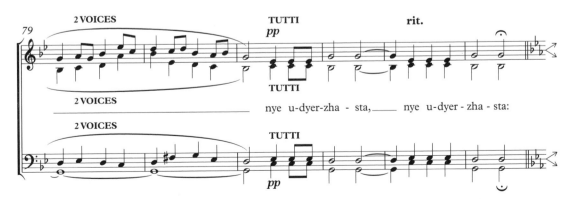

* The SAT tutti voices should stop on the first beat of bar 77, while the solo voices continue.

poco meno mosso (Nemnogo medlennee)

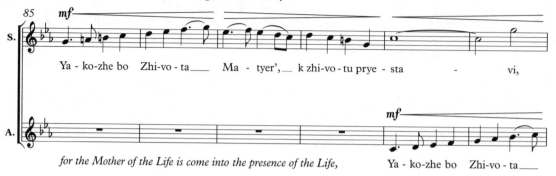

Ya - ko-zhe bo Zhi-vo - ta___ Ma - tyer',___ k zhi-vo-tu prye - sta - vi,

for the Mother of the Life is come into the presence of the Life, Ya - ko-zhe bo Zhi-vo - ta___

Ma - tyer',___ k zhi-vo-tu prye - sta - vi,___ k zhi-vo-tu___ prye-sta -

Ma - tyer',___ k zhi-vo-tu prye - sta - vi, Ma - tyer',___ k zhi-vo - tu prye -

Ya - ko-zhe bo Zhi-vo - ta___ Ma - tyer',___ k zhi-vo - tu prye -

* Keyboard reduction for rehearsal only.

who took up his abode in her ever-virgin womb.

-li - vïy-sya pri - sno - dyev-stvyen-nu-yu, vo u-tro-bu Vsye-li - vïy-sya

pri - sno - dyev-stvyen-nu-yu, pri - sno - dyev - stvyen-nu - yu,____

a tempo

vo u tro-bu Vsye-li - vïy-sya pri - sno - dyev-stvyen-nu-yu, vo u-tro-bu Vsye-

-li - vïy-sya pri - sno - dyev-stvyen-nu-yu, pri-sno - dyev - stvyen-nu - yu.

26. The Great Doxology
(*Slavosloviye vyelikoye*)

All-night Vigil

PAVEL CHESNOKOV
(1877–1944)
Op. 44 No. 9

Glory be to God on high, and on earth peace,

good will towards men.

We praise thee, we bless thee, we worship thee, we glorify thee,

we give thanks to thee for thy great glory.

-li - ki-ya ra - di sla-vï Tvo-ye - ya.

-li - ki-ya ra - di sla-vï Tvo-ye - ya.

-li - ki-ya ra - di sla-vï Tvo-ye - ya,___ sla-vï Tvo-ye - ya.

-li - ki-ya ra - di sla-vï Tvo-ye - ya, sla - vï Tvo-ye - ya.

Prayerful (Molitvenno)

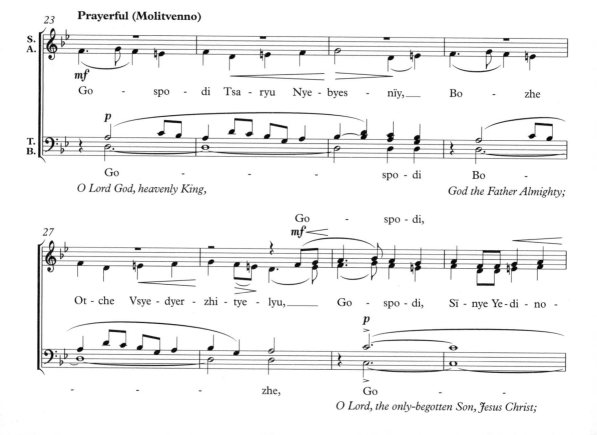

Go - spo - di Tsa-ryu Nye-byes - nïy,___ Bo - zhe

Go - - - - spo - di Bo -

O Lord God, heavenly King,   *God the Father Almighty;*

Go - spo - di,

Ot - che Vsye-dyer - zhi-tye - lyu,___ Go - spo - di, Sï - nye Ye-di - no -

- - - - zhe, Go - -

O Lord, the only-begotten Son, Jesus Christ;

Du - she.

-rod - nïy, I - i - su - sye Khri - stye, i Svya - tïy___ Du - she.

-spo - di, I - i - su - sye Khri - stye,___

and Holy Spirit.

mf

Go - spo - di Bo-zhe, Agn-che Bo - zhïy, Sï - nye O - tyech, Vzyem - lyay gryekh

p

Go - - - - - spo - di, Vzyem -

O Lord God, Lamb of God, Son of the Father,   *that takest away the sins*

move progressively from contemplation/supplication to acclamation

S.   *mf*

vzyem - lyay grye-khi mi-ra, pri-i-mi mo-

A.   *mf*

mi - ra, po - mi - luy_ nas; vzyem - lyay___ pri - i -

T.   *mf*

lyay,___ vzyem - lyay grye-khi mi-ra, pri-i-mi mo-

B.

lyay, vzyem - lyay___ pri - i -

mf

of the world, have mercy upon us;   *thou that takest away the sins of the world, receive our prayer.*

Thou that sittest at the right hand of the Father, have mercy upon us;

for thou only art holy;   *thou only art the Lord,*

Jesus Christ,   *to the glory of God the Father.*

Amen.

Calm... prayerful glorification (Tikho... molitvenno slavoslovia)

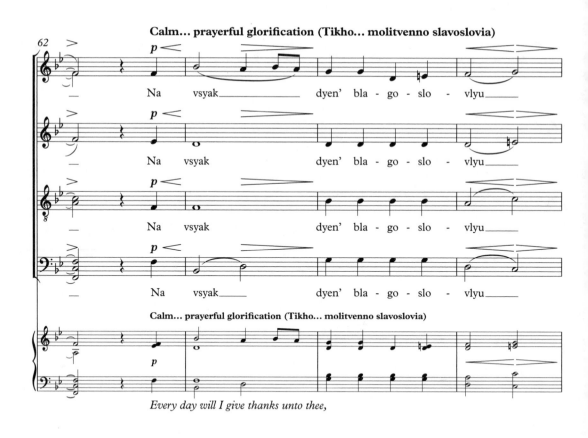

Every day will I give thanks unto thee,

and praise thy name for ever and ever.

Move progressively towards a majestic glorification

Vouchsafe, O Lord, to keep us this day without sin.

Blessed art thou, O Lord God of our fathers,

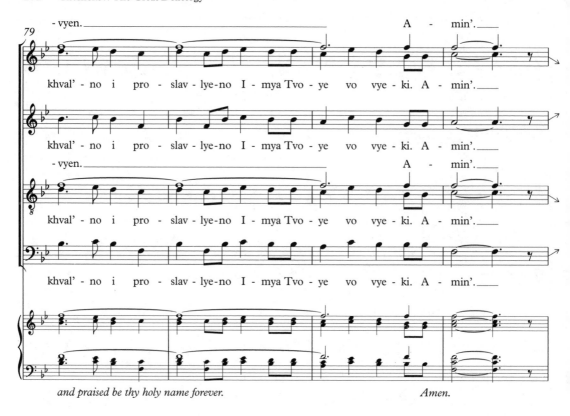

and praised be thy holy name forever.   Amen.

Calm, prayerful (Tikho, molitvenno)

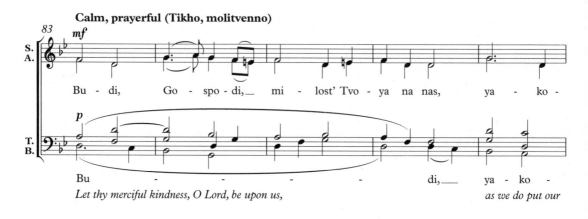

Let thy merciful kindness, O Lord, be upon us,   as we do put our

trust in thee.   Blessed art thou, O Lord,

Lord, thou hast been our refuge from one generation to another.

I said: Lord, be merciful unto me,

heal my soul,   for I have sinned against thee.   Lord, I flee unto thee.

Teach me to do the things that pleaseth thee,

move progressively from contemplation to glorification

for thou art my God: *for with thee is the well of life;*

and in thy light we shall see light.

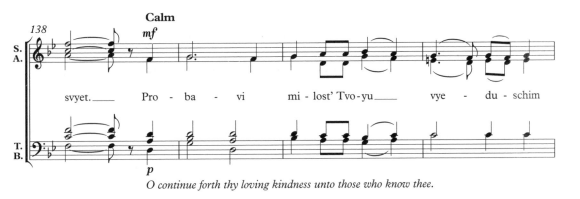

svyet._____ Pro - ba - vi   mi - lost' Tvo - yu_____   vye - du - schim

O continue forth thy loving kindness unto those who know thee.

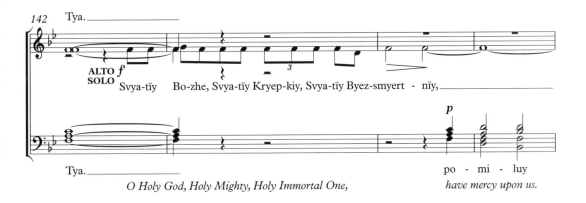

Tya._____

ALTO SOLO *f* Svya-tïy   Bo-zhe, Svya-tïy Kryep-kiy, Svya-tïy Byez-smyert - nïy,_____   *p* po - mi - luy

Tya._____

O Holy God, Holy Mighty, Holy Immortal One,   *have mercy upon us.*

Svya-tïy   Bo-zhe, Svya-tïy Kryep-kiy, Svya-tïy Byez-smyert - nïy,_____   *p* po - mi - luy

nas._____

Svya-tïy   Bo-zhe, Svya-tïy Kryep-kiy, Svya-tïy Byez-smyert - nïy,_____   *p* po - mi - luy

nas._____

Sla - va Ot-tsu, i Sï-nu, i Svya-to-mu Du-khu, i nï-nye i pri-sno i vo vye - ki vye-

nas.____

Glory to the Father, and to the Son, and to the Holy Spirit, both now and ever, and unto ages of ages.

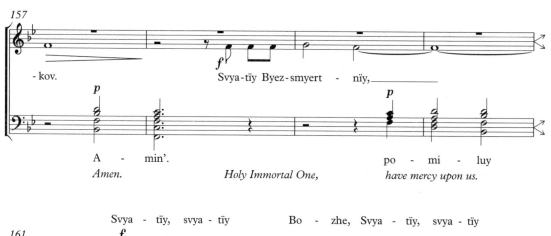

- kov.   Svya-tïy Byez-smyert - nïy,____

A - min'.   po - mi - luy

Amen.   *Holy Immortal One,*   *have mercy upon us.*

O Holy God,   *Holy Mighty,*

Holy Immortal One,   *have mercy upon us.*

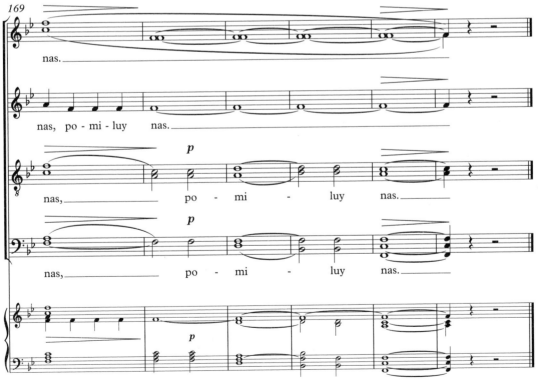

180

27. The Great Doxology
(*Slavosloviye vyelikoye No. 2*)

All-night Vigil

ALEXANDER KASTALSKY
(1856–1926)

we bless thee, we worship thee,   we glorify thee,

we give thanks to thee for thy great glory.

O Lord, heavenly King,   God the Father Almighty;

Go - spo - di, Sï - nye Ye - di - no - rod - nïy,___ I - i -
- spo - - - - - spo

O Lord, the only-begotten Son, Jesus Christ;

Du - she, Go - spo - di.

- su - sye Khri-stye, i Svya - tïy___ Du - she.___
- - - - - di.

and Holy Spirit.

a tempo

Go - spo-di Bo-zhe, Agn-che Bo - zhïy, Sï - nye O-tyech, Vzyem-lyay gryekh mi - ra, po-mi - luy

Go - spo - di Sï - nye O - tyech,___ po-mi - luy

Go - spo-di Bo-zhe, Agn-che Bo - zhïy, Sï - nye O-tyech, Vzyem-lyay gryekh mi - ra, po-mi - luy

O Lord God, Lamb of God, Son of the Father,   *that takest away the sins of the world, have mercy upon us;*

nas,___ po - mi -

nas, po - mi - luy nas; vzyem-lyay grye-khi mi - ra, pri - i - mi mo - li - tvu na - shu. Sye -

thou that takest away the sins of the world, receive our prayer.

Thou that sittest at the right hand of the Father, have mercy upon us;   for thou only art holy;

thou only art the Lord, Jesus Christ,   to the glory of

God the Father.   Amen.   Every day will I give thanks unto thee,

and praise thy name for ever and ever.

tempo I

- ka.   Bla - go - slo -

do - bi,   byez grye - kha   so - khra - ni - ti - sya nam.

- do - bi,   Go - spo - di,   v dyen syey

Vouchsafe, O Lord, to keep us this day without sin.

- vyen, bla - go - slo - vyen_____   ye - si,   i

Bla - go - slo - vyen_ ye - si,____   Go - spo - di, Bo - zhe o - tyets_ na - shikh, i

Blessed art thou, O Lord, the God of our fathers,

khval' - no i_ pro - slav - lye - no_   I - mya Tvo - ye____   vo_

and praised be thy holy name forever.

rit.   **a tempo**

vye - ki. A - min'.   Bu - di,_ Go - spo - di, mi lost' Tvo-ya na

Bu - di,   Go - spo - di,   mi lost' Tvo - ya na nas,

Amen.   Let thy merciful kindness, O Lord, be upon us,

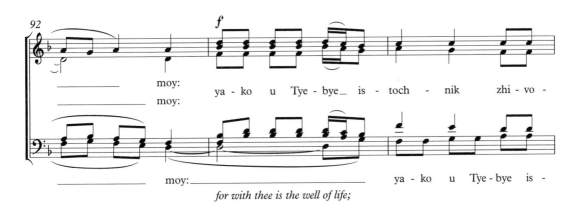

moy:
moy:
ya - ko u Tye - bye_ is - toch - nik zhi - vo -
moy:_____ ya - ko u Tye - bye is -

for with thee is the well of life;

Pro -
- ta,_____ vo svye - tye Tvo - yem_ u - zrim_ svyet. Pro -
- toch - nik zhi - vo - ta, vo

and in thy light we shall see light.

- ba - vi, pro - ba - vi
- ba - vi mi - lost' Tvo - yu_ vye - du - schim Tya.

O continue forth thy loving kindness unto those who know thee.

do not slow down (ne zatyagivaya tempa)

Svya - tïy_____ Bo - zhe, Svya - tïy_____ Kryep - kiy,
O Holy God, *Holy Mighty,*

Svya - tïy___ Byez - smyert - nïy, po - mi - luy nas.

Holy Immortal One,   have mercy upon us.

espressivo

Svya - tïy_____ Bo - zhe,___ Svya - tïy_____ Kryep - kiy,

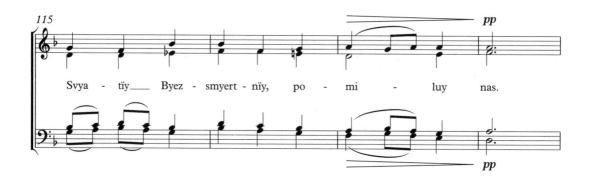

Svya - tïy___ Byez - smyert - nïy, po - mi - luy nas.

Svya - tïy_____ Bo - zhe, Svya - tïy_____ Kryep - kiy,

Glory to the Father, and to the Son, and to the Holy Spirit,   *both now and ever,*

and unto ages of ages.   *Amen.*

Holy Immortal One,   *have mercy upon us.*

NOTES ON THE COMPOSERS AND THEIR WORKS

Alexander Arkhangelsky (1846–1924) was born into the family of a priest in the village of Staroe Tezikovo near Penza, and received his education at the Penza Theological Seminary. He later obtained a diploma in choral conducting from the Imperial Chapel in St Petersburg, and from 1873 worked as a conductor with various choirs in the city. In 1880, he became the first conductor to establish a choir with women's voices rather than boys'. His mixed choir, considered among the best in the country, sang in churches and concert halls throughout Russia and abroad, performing European masterpieces, Russian liturgical music, and folk-song arrangements by Arkhangelsky himself. After the 1917 Revolution, the Arkhangelsky choir was renamed as the State Academic Choir, and was conducted by its founder for the last time in December 1921. From 1922, Arkhangelsky lived in Prague, where he died in 1924. The Penza College of Music now takes the name of its famous former resident.

As a composer, Arkhangelsky was known for his church music. He wrote two settings of the Liturgy, an All-night Vigil, and many smaller-scale pieces to be performed during Communion. Along with composers Grigory Lvovsky, Alexei Lvov, Nikolai Rimsky-Korsakov, and Mily Balakirev, he belonged to the St Petersburg School of Russian sacred music. In contrast to the Moscow School, these composers did not insist on using traditional chants as the one and only criteria of spirituality (although Arkhangelsky did make some arrangements of *znamenny* chant), and instead freely applied the principles of Western polyphony to their work. Their compositions, with all their charm, do not therefore sound so unmistakably Russian.

'**I Cry Aloud With My Voice Unto the Lord**' is a setting of Psalm 142, which is frequently read in the Orthodox Church at the service of Fervent Supplication. Arkhangelsky's version belongs to the category of the sacred concerto, which can be performed in the Liturgy during the priests' Communion, for which there are no 'set' pieces, and at concerts of sacred music.

Maxim Berezovsky (1745–77) received his singing training, and probably was born, in Glukhov in Ukraine (at that time known as Malorussia). Glukhov was renowned for producing fine singers, and the Imperial Chapel and other choirs in St Petersburg often recruited their choristers from the region. In 1759, Berezovsky was invited to join the choir of Prince Pyotr Fedorovich, and in 1762 he became a member of the Imperial Chapel. Alongside his singing, he studied composition with the Italian masters living in Russia at the time (primarily Baldassare Galuppi), and wrote many sacred works. 'He composed superlative church concertos for the Imperial Chapel with such taste and such outstanding harmony that the performances provoked the connoisseur's delight and the royal court's approval', wrote Jacob von Stählin in his *Nachtichten von der Musik in Russland* ('News about Music in Russia', 1769).

In *c.*1765, Berezovsky travelled to Italy to study with renowned teacher Padre Giovanni Battista Marini at the Bologna Philharmonic Academy. He graduated with distinction, and became an honourary member of the academia. Upon his return to St Petersburg in 1774, he was appointed as a Kapellmeister of the Imperial Chapel. His premature death at the age of 32 gave rise to rumours of suicide. However, so little is known about him that no such suggestion can be accepted with any certainty. Recent discoveries of Berezovsky's secular works (his Symphony in C from the 1770s was discovered in the Vatican archives in 2002) demonstrate his great artistic gift, which arguably has not yet been fully appreciated.

Berezovsky became the first great master of the sacred concerto, a Classical-style choral work blending the traditions of Russian *a cappella* church singing with those of the choral psalm motet of the Venetian and Bolognese schools. Sadly, only three of Berezovsky's eighteen known concertos have been located. The greatest is the concerto for four voices, '**Do Not Reject Me in My Old Age**' (Psalm 71: 9–13), which was composed before 1769. The work can be divided into four sections: the slow introit, reflecting the grief and despair of the opening words; the 'evil fugato' of the *turbae* from bar 48; the adagio prayer 'Bozhe moy' ('O my God') from bar 124; and the fugal section from bar 145, reflecting the hope for revenge and deliverance. The tragic emotional intensity of this masterpiece ensured its role in the development of Russian music, both sacred and secular.

Dmitry Bortniansky (1751–1825), known as the master of Russian Classicism, was born into the family of a Ukrainian Cossack. He received his first musical training in Glukhov, Ukraine, before being sent to St Petersburg at the age of 7 to sing at the Imperial Chapel, where he studied theory and composition with Baldassare Galuppi. In 1768, at his teacher's recommendation, he travelled to Venice, where he wrote his first operas, cantatas, and sonatas. On his return to St Petersburg in 1779 he was appointed as a Kapellmeister in the Imperial Chapel, and in 1796 became Director, retaining that influential position until his death in 1825. Under his directorship, the Imperial Chapel became one of the finest choirs in Europe.

A prolific composer, Bortniansky produced over a hundred works for the church, among them ten concertos for double choir, thirty-five four-part concertos, and several settings of the Liturgy. His unique choral style gained many admirers across Europe, both during his lifetime and after his death. Writing in his diary during a trip to Russia in 1847, Berlioz praised Bortniansky's 'rare skills of arranging choral resources, wonderful combinations of nuances, and extremely rich harmonies'. However, others criticized Bortniansky for his 'blind' adherence to the foreign school and the excessive sentimentality of his music.

In fact, Bortniansky was one of the first to speak out about the necessity of returning Russian sacred music to its roots. Years after Bortniansky's death, Stepan Smolensky proved that the composer was behind the anonymous 'Project on printing ancient Russian neumatic singing', published in 1810 (later known as 'Bortniansky's Project'). At the time, when fashion dominated lives, Bortniansky was compelled to produce compositions in the popular style and manner that was expected from him. In his free time, however, he harmonized traditional chants. 'He had enough intellect and tact to sort out infatuations of his time, to master the science of foreign music, and to understand the true road for Russian music—the need to return to the native chants', wrote Smolensky in his essay *In memory of Bortniansky* (1901). '**Many Years**' is one such example, in which the traditional tune is preserved without a change. This short piece can hardly bear witness to those qualities of Bortniansky's music that Berlioz so admired, yet it is significant in demonstrating an initial return to the harmonization of traditional chants.

Pavel Chesnokov (1877–1944) was born in Voskresensk, near Moscow, where his father was a church choir conductor. Musically gifted as a boy, he attended the Moscow Synodal School, from where he graduated in 1885 with a gold medal. He studied composition with Stepan Smolensky ('my first and most important teacher') and later with Sergei Taneyev. Chesnokov's first compositions, written while he was still at school, were immediately successful, and he continued composing while working as a conductor and teacher. Already an established composer and choir director, he became a student at the Moscow Conservatoire at the age of 36, where he strived to improve his mastery of composition even further. A younger representative of the New Direction, Chesnokov followed in the footsteps of Kastalsky and Grechaninov. Like Kastalsky, he treated traditional chants with utmost respect and, like Grechaninov, aspired to 'symphonize' the sound of the choir, achieving his own variety of 'orchestral' tone colours within his choral music. By 1917 he was acknowledged as a giant of Russian sacred music.

After the Revolution, many of Chesnokov's friends and colleagues emigrated, including his brother Alexander, who was also a composer. Chesnokov remained in Russia and continued conducting church music; he was the choir director at the Cathedral of Christ the Saviour in Moscow until it was demolished in 1931. At the same time, he tried to integrate into the life of the new Soviet Union and conducted, among other secular groups, the choir of the Bolshoi Theatre, as well as teaching at the Moscow Conservatoire. However, these secular positions were limited, for his continuing involvement with the church meant that he was never considered entirely loyal to the new regime.

In 1940, after years of delay, Chesnokov's book *Khor i upravlenie im* ('The Choir and How to Direct It'), dedicated to Smolensky, was authorized for publication. Reflecting the vast experience of its author, the book was designed as a theoretical foundation and encyclopedia for young conductors. It proved very popular and was reprinted several times. Somewhat tellingly, this famous conductor of sacred music referred only once to a sacred work: Maxim Berezovsky's 'Do Not Reject Me in My Old Age'. Such was the price to pay for publication.

Setting a text from the All-night Vigil, **'Blessed is the Man'** (Op. 11 No. 2) was composed in 1907 and is an arrangement of the so-called Greek chant, which takes its origin in seventeenth-century Russia (see Appendix Ia, page 200). From a similar period (*c*.1910) is the **Cherubic Hymn** (Op. 33 No. 6), which sets words from the Liturgy to the chant known as 'The Repentant Thief' (see Appendix Ib, page 201). Both works represent Chesnokov's early style, which is simpler and more archaic in spirit than that of his later output. They demonstrate the composer's knowledge of traditional chants, as well as his considerable skill in arranging an existing melody in a tactful yet musically interesting way. **'Lord, Save the Faithful'** and **Trisagion**, Op. 38 No. 1, is another of Chesnokov's earlier works (*c*.1912), written before he attended the Moscow Conservatoire. Many of his original compositions could be described as expressive and even somewhat sentimental (especially in contrast to Kastalsky), yet the melody of this particular piece is much closer in style to that of a Russian folk song. The **Great Doxology**, Op. 44 No. 9, is from the All-night Vigil cycle of 1915—one of Chesnokov's greatest works, demonstrating a more mature, elaborate style.

Nikolai Golovanov (1891–1953), the son of a tailor, was born in Moscow. He received a free education at the Moscow Synodal School, where he was a boy soloist in the choir, and it was here that his first compositions were performed. He continued his studies at the Moscow Conservatoire and additionally with Mikhail Ippolitov-Ivanov.

From 1915 Golovanov worked at the Bolshoi Theatre, first as a choir master and later as chief conductor. In 1928 he was accused of conservatism and 'bourgeois moralism', and was dismissed from his position. The campaign against him, known as *Golovanshchina* ('the Golovanov case'), was widely followed by the press, and served as a warning to others. He returned to the Bolshoi as chief conductor between 1948 and 1953, where he performed well-known masterpieces and premiered works by Prokofiev, Shostakovich, Myaskovsky, Khrennikov, and others. He was awarded four Stalin Prizes, as well as many other medals and titles.

Despite all the risks, Golovanov remained an Orthodox Christian throughout his life, and his sacred works were among the last to be published before the Revolution. He played an important part in preserving the archives of the Moscow Synodal School (sadly the greater part of the library has now perished), saved many items associated with church rituals (which he disguised as his 'art collection'), gave financial help to Archbishop Trifon Turkestanov, and supported church conductors and composers, including Danilin and Chesnokov. Many of his sacred works, including his setting of **'Our Father'** (Op. 9 No. 3), demonstrate his affiliation with composers of the New Direction (indeed, many of his compositions are dedicated to Smolensky and Kastalsky).

Golovanov composed several symphonic works, two operas, over two hundred romances, and many folk-song arrangements. He was married to the legendary Russian soprano Antonina Nezhdanova and often performed as her piano accompanist.

Alexander Grechaninov (1864–1956) was born into the family of a Moscow merchant, who had relocated from the provincial town of Kaluga. Despite coming to music rather late (he claimed to have not set eyes on a piano until the age of 14), and against his father's will, he went on to graduate as a pianist and composer from the Moscow and St Petersburg Conservatoires respectively. Grechaninov was determined to pursue the idea of Russianness in his music, and his first symphonies and romances, and the opera *Dobrïnya Nikitich*, bear witness to this. From 1903 he was actively involved with the Music Ethnographic Society at Moscow University, where he enjoyed researching Russian folklore.

Having had a religious upbringing, Grechaninov was naturally inclined towards composing for the church. From 1897, he developed a close friendship and collaboration with Stepan Smolensky, the Director of the Moscow Synodal School, and the composer often had the opportunity to hear his new works performed by the Synodal Choir and to make adjustments where necessary. He also contributed profusely to discussions in the press on the questions of spirituality and nationality in music.

Grechaninov enjoyed his position of popularity with the Russian royal family. His songs were performed by the Empress and, on Tsar Nicholas II's orders, his setting of the Credo was sung at court every Sunday. Conversely, his *Hymn of Free Russia*, composed after the events of February 1917 and the abdication of the Tsar, was widely praised. Although Grechaninov was initially determined to stay in his motherland, the chaos and hardships of the civil war proved too much. In 1925 he left Russia for France, and in 1939 emigrated to the United States. His memoirs, entitled *My Life*, were published first in Paris and later in New York.

Grechaninov was a prolific composer of both sacred and secular music. Among his works are five symphonies, six operas (three for children), orchestral works, sonatas for various instruments, cantatas, and over two hundred songs (he has been dubbed 'the Russian Schubert'). Yet Grechaninov considered himself primarily a composer of sacred music, and it was this genre in particular (including Orthodox liturgical music, Catholic masses, Protestant hymns, and works in Hebrew) that brought him fame both in Russia and abroad.

Two of Grechaninov's most celebrated achievements are his settings of the 'Passion Week' (*Strastnaya Sedmitsa*, Op. 58, 1911) and the All-night Vigil (Op. 59, 1912). Combining Russian antiquity and European Renaissance textures, his compositional style in these two cycles is sometimes described as Russian Choral Neo-Baroque. Grechaninov himself referred to his extremely colourful and rich part-writing as the 'symphonization of the choir'.

As with some other pieces in the Op. 59 All-night Vigil cycle, '**Bless the Lord, O My Soul**' (Op. 59 No. 1) is designed with a multi-layered structure: at the *Poco meno mosso* (bar 26), the choir continues to sing the main melody and text while a group of soloists begins a new motif, providing a contrast by picturing the 'waters upon the mountains'. The dividing of the choir in such a way hints at the Orthodox tradition of using two choirs antiphonally (as described in the Old Testament). One of the highlights of the All-night Vigil cycle, the majestic '**Praise the Name of the Lord**' (Op. 59 No. 5) is reminiscent of Russian liturgical and folk singing, though it is entirely original. Also setting a text from the All-night Vigil, Grechaninov's '**Gentle Light**' (Op. 23 No. 2) is an earlier work, from 1900, that already exhibits the lush chordal writing characteristic of his future 'symphonic' style.

Taken from Grechaninov's second setting of the Liturgy, '**It is Truly Meet**' (Op. 29 No. 10, 1902), is a simple and diatonic harmonization of the old *demestvenny* chant; only the majestic ending in a different tonality discloses the fact that the composer was searching for new paths in his choral writing. In contrast, the next work in the Liturgy cycle, '**Our Father**' (Op. 29 No. 11), is an original composition in the style of Russian antiquity. The second Liturgy established Grechaninov as one of the leading exponents of the New Direction.

Viktor Kalinnikov (1870–1927) was born in the Russian district of Mtsensk, into the family of a policeman. He studied at the Oryol Theological Seminary and later the Moscow College of Music and Drama, and upon graduation taught music and conducted the orchestra at the college. In 1897 he joined the teaching staff at the Moscow Synodal School, and from 1922 was a professor of music theory at the Moscow Conservatoire. Kalinnikov began composing while at the Synodal School, where he was greatly influenced by the ideas of the New Direction. Unlike other representatives of the movement, Kalinnikov rarely used traditional chants, but instead created his own melodies using the characteristic features of Russian liturgical music. As well as sacred works, Kalinnikov composed much secular choral music based on Russian literature, including many songs for children. His brother Vasily Kalinnikov, also a composer, followed the traditions of the Mighty Handful, and wrote mostly secular music in the national style, including two symphonies.

'**Rejoice, O Virgin Mother of God**' (All-night Vigil) is based on words from St Luke's Gospel. Here Kalinnikov creates his own style, combining melodic elements characteristic of Russian liturgical chants and folk songs.

Alexander Kastalsky (1856–1926) was born in Moscow, where his father was a much-respected archpriest and writer, and the founder of a diocesan college for women. Having graduated from the Moscow Conservatoire, Kastalsky worked for some time as a music teacher in the provincial town of Kozlov (now Michurinsk). Upon his return to Moscow in 1886 he taught at the Moscow Synodal School, where he stayed for thirty-seven years; in 1903 he became the conductor of the Synodal Choir, and in 1910 was made Director. He began studying and harmonizing traditional chants under the guidance of Stepan Smolensky, and his first experimental compositions at the age of 40 exceeded all expectations. After the Revolution, Kastalsky had a choice: to leave his homeland or to integrate into the new Soviet society. He accepted an invitation to teach at the Moscow Conservatoire, and continued composing, but from that point onwards he concentrated mostly on secular music in the style of Russian folk song. He was described by some as 'the Red Professor'.

Kastalsky composed a broad spectrum of over four hundred sacred compositions, from a multitude of common liturgical hymns to majestic works for festive services and special occasions. Among his secular works are an opera (*Klara Milich*), several cantatas, and numerous works for children, most of which were based on Russian literature and folklore. Despite his full-time job as a teacher, he left a substantial legacy not only in music but also in other fields: poetry, articles, letters, memoirs, and many paintings.

Kastalsky's guiding compositional principle was to free Russian music from the yoke of Europeanism. As with other composers of the New Direction, he battled with the pivotal issue of how to harmonize traditional monodic chants. His answer was to develop the theory and practice of 'national counterpoint', which involved applying the *podgolosok* polyphony of Russian folk singing to sacred music (see page vii). Later on, the reputation of Kastalsky was such that the New Direction was often described 'Kastalsky's Direction'.

Written in 1898, '**A Mercy of Peace**' (Divine Liturgy) was one of Kastalsky's first attempts at harmonizing *znamenny* chant using *podgolosok* polyphony. In this work, the choir responds to phrases chanted by the clergy, the words of which are presented in the score. Although the meaning of the sung text is technically incomplete without the words of the Deacon/Celebrant, it is not uncommon for concert performances to include only the choral parts. Alternatively, the chanted parts may be performed by a member of the choir, possibly omitting lines 6–8, either on a monotone (usually the tonic or dominant) or using a more elaborate style of intonation.

The **Cherubic Hymn** (Divine Liturgy) is based on a popular anonymous chant that goes back to the seventeenth century and was later called 'The Ravaging of Moscow' (*Na razoryeniye Moskvï*) in remembrance of the devastation of Moscow by the French in 1812. It was Smolensky who brought the tune to Kastalsky's attention in 1898, encouraging him to use the style of Russian antiquity to give it an artistic form. Like 'A Mercy of Peace', the Cherubic Hymn was one of Kastalsky's first harmonizations in this style.

In 1903–4, Kastalsky wrote several pieces for the All-night Vigil service, and '**Gentle Light**' was set three times. No. 3, the most festive and emotionally powerful setting, opens with the upper voices, with men reciting the text beneath. The gentle and elegiac melodic material representing Christ is followed by the solemn glorification of the Redeemer by the whole choir, creating a powerful effect reminiscent of Russian church bells ringing.

Among the last works of the 1904 All-night Vigil cycle were two versions of the **Great Doxology No. 2** (one for large choir, included here, and one for small choir), based on *znamenny* chant in a major tonality. Many of the choral devices typical of Kastalsky can be found in this piece: interchanges between choral groups and brilliant 'orchestral' tuttis for the whole choir, low 'pedals' in the basses, rapid choral reciting, and sonorous fanfares in same-voice parts. This work is an example of how the composer treated a lengthy and capricious *znamenny* chant melody while preserving its originality. Kastalsky was the first of the New Direction composers to complete a choral All-night Vigil setting, and his work paved the way for the others.

Nicolas Ossorguine (b. 1924) and **Nikolai Kedrov Jr** (1905–81) represent the many Russians who were brought up outside their homeland, after both families emigrated to France following the Revolution. Like his father Mikhail, Nicolas Ossorguine taught at the St Sergius Orthodox Theological Institute in Paris, and was a choir director and an expert in traditional chants. Kedrov's father, Nikolai Kedrov Sr, was a well-known opera singer before the Revolution, performing in both the Bolshoi and the Mariinsky Theatres, and taught at the St Petersburg Conservatoire. In 1897 he founded a male-voice vocal quartet, which was highly successful throughout Russia and abroad, and the group continued to perform after the family's relocation in 1922. Kedrov Jr headed the quartet following his father's death, and the ensemble has continued under the direction of Kedrov's descendents.

Ossorguine and Kedrov Jr collaborated in harmonizing traditional monodic chants, continuing the traditions of the Moscow School outside Russia. In 2008, at the conference 'Russian Diaspora: Music and Orthodoxy', Patriarch Kirill commented that it was thanks to such émigrés that 'Russian sacred music in the Diaspora was not only preserved, but developed, revealing to the non-Orthodox the magnificence and beauty of Holy Orthodoxy'.

'**It is Truly Meet**', from the Liturgy, is a harmonization of an anonymous *znamenny* chant (see Appendix Ic, page 202). One of the most ancient and complete Russian chants, *znamenny* is now the symbol of the Orthodox Church and is often called 'theology in sound'. The name comes from the word *znamya*, meaning 'neuma'—a sign depicting the music in plainchant notation. The original *znamenny* chant had a special system of neumatic notation, which was developed under the influence of Byzantine notation and later became independent. *Znamenny* melodies are known for their smooth, step-like movement and free asymmetrical rhythms. They are diatonic, yet the absence of an underlying scale and a definite tonic makes it difficult to define the prevailing mood.

Sergei Prokofiev (1891–1953) enriched Russian culture with the innovative music of his ballets, operas, symphonies, piano compositions, and settings of words by great poets. He was also interested in Russian folklore, as demonstrated by his ballets *The Tale of the Buffoon* and *The Tale of the Stone Flower*, as well as his attractive arrangements of Russian folk songs. Another prominent theme in Prokofiev's music is history: he wrote symphonic suites for the films *Alexander Nevsky* and *Ivan the Terrible*, the opera *War and Peace*, and the cantatas *Alexander Nevsky* and *For the 20th Anniversary of the October Revolution*. Sacred music was the only area that he did not touch.

Having left Russia for the USA in 1918, Prokofiev finally returned to the USSR in 1936 as a celebrity, known both in Europe and America. While he conformed to the Communist ideology, he later found that his creativity was limited by the strict Soviet censorship. He still managed to experiment with tradition and modernity in his music, but this often resulted in oppressive criticism by the authorities.

'Many Years' was written as part of the film score for *Ivan the Terrible* (1945). Following their productive partnership on the film *Alexander Nevsky*, the famous producer Sergei Eisenstein invited Prokofiev to collaborate once again in 1942. The film was described by the press as 'a music and cinema epic', and its great success was due to a large extent to its captivating music. Though not sacred music in the traditional sense of the word, but rather a historic illustration, 'Many Years' sounds entirely authentic, revealing Prokofiev's ability to master different styles.

Sergei Rakhmaninov (1873–1943) remains one of the most well-known and widely performed composers of his age. An unparalleled concert pianist, he contributed a substantial and important body of works to the piano repertory, including numerous preludes and sonatas and three concertos, and his momentous symphonic works have proved to be equally significant in the orchestral canon. Rakhmaninov left Russia following the Revolution, spending the rest of his life in Europe and America, although he never lost sight of the customs and traditions of his Russian upbringing.

Highly secretive, Rakhmaninov always kept his religious views to himself. However, his setting of the Liturgy of 1910 was the first to which he added the epigraph 'Thanks be to God', suggesting that by that time he may have considered himself as religious in outlook if not in strict practice. Rakhmaninov composed a number of other Orthodox works, including a setting of the All-night Vigil, which has arguably become the best-known work in the Russian Orthodox repertoire. Written in 1915, when the composer was at the height of his fame, the Vigil was eagerly awaited by all lovers of sacred music and supporters of the New Direction, for it was known that Rakhmaninov was under the influence of the Moscow School. Indeed, the work was dedicated to Stepan Smolensky, with whom Rakhmaninov studied the traditional chants.

'The Ever-Vigilant Mother of God' was written in 1893, well before the young composer was influenced by the ideas of the New Direction (he first met with Smolensky in 1897). It is a composition in a free style—possibly just an exercise in part-writing following the *a cappella* motet *Deus meus*, which was Rakhmaninov's counterpoint examination piece at the Moscow Conservatoire. The text is a *kontakion* (a short hymn) from the service commemorating the Dormition of the Mother of God (the 'falling asleep' of Mary, or the Assumption in the Western tradition).

Alfred Schnittke (1934–98) was born into a Jewish–German family in the Russian city of Engels on the Volga river. He travelled widely during his lifetime, spending his early years studying in Vienna and much of his later life in Hamburg, but always considered himself to be a Russian composer. He graduated from the Moscow Conservertoire in 1961, and went on to teach there until 1972. Schnittke's early composing career revolved around the Soviet film industry, securing him a good income and reputation while also allowing him the freedom to work on other compositional genres. He was one of the last to pursue the great symphonic tradition, taking influence from Mahler and Shostakovich. In the 1970s and 80s he enjoyed enormous popularity in Russia, and he gradually became one of the most prominent composers of the second half of the twentieth century.

Schnittke had a great interest in the mystical traditions of different religions, including Kaballah and I Ching, and this influenced much of his work. He first quoted from traditional Russian chants in his four *Hymns* for solo cello and instrumental ensemble (1979), and went on to use the chants more frequently in his later works. In his Fourth Symphony (1983), he reconciled his religious dilemma by using Christian chants from different traditions as well as Jewish melodies. His intense spiritual search eventually led him to Christianity and, although the Orthodox Church was to become his spiritual home, he took the decision to be baptized in a Catholic church in Vienna in 1982. The somewhat shocking clashes of his style and the symbolism of his music remain the subject of many discussions.

In 1984, in a single night, Schnittke composed his *Three Sacred Songs*, setting texts from the Divine Liturgy; '**Our Father**' is the third in the set. Though original, the songs are very close in mood and style to genuine Russian Orthodox music.

Georgy Sviridov (1915–98), the son of a postman and a teacher, was born in the Russian province of Kursk. As a young boy he fell in love with the balalaika and, encouraged by his school teachers, enrolled at the Leningrad Conservatoire, where he studied composition with Shostakovich and graduated in 1941 as a pianist and composer. Vocal music (both choral and solo) became his favourite compositional genre; passionate about Russian literature, he set to music the works of some of Russia's finest poets, including Pushkin, Lermontov, Yesenin, Blok, Mayakovsky, and Tvardovsky.

Sviridov's prize-spangled career as a great Soviet artist may suggest that he was an 'official composer'—one of the cogs in the Communist wheel. The truth is not so black and white. While he did compose monuments in the style of 'socialist realism', at the same time he wrote what he wanted, expressing his attachment to Russia's slavic roots, and was a leading figure in the 'new folklore trend' of the mid-1960s. The Communist ideology prohibited the composition of sacred music, so Sviridov cleverly disguised his works under a historic theme. In his later years, he was able to compose more for the church, and his sacred compositions are a logical continuation of the choral tradition of the Moscow School.

'**Sacred Love**' is the second of the *Three Choruses*, written in 1973, from the incidental music for Tolstoy's play *Tsar Feodor Ioannovich* (the story of a kind and sensitive man who is unable to become the 'proper' ruler of the country). This chorus, unlike the other two, sets a non-liturgical text. Its chant-like melody is carried by soprano solo over a drone in the other voices.

Pyotr Tchaikovsky (1840–93) has become one of the most popular and well-known composers of all time, with a vast catalogue of works that includes symphonies, concertos, operas, chamber music, songs, and compositions for piano. Tchaikovsky enjoyed attending services of the Orthodox Church and had a great passion for its music. He was a zealous campaigner for the revival of traditional Russian chants, and when the New Direction assumed its definitive shape, Tchaikovsky was proclaimed as one of its founders. In 1878, he wrote a letter to the Metropolitan of Kiev:

> As a result of fatal circumstances, the abominable, sugary sweet, and over-sentimental style was forced into our church, and our sacred music is currently in a most miserable state. As a musician and as an Orthodox Christian, I cannot be satisfied with this situation, regardless of how beautiful and well balanced are the singers' voices, regardless of how masterly is the conductor. We have after all the traditional chants, which are not only musically beautiful but also highly original.

Right up until his death, he followed the activities of the Moscow Synodal School and Choir with great interest, and was a member of the Supervisory Council attached to the school.

Tchaikovsky's first work for the church—his setting of the Divine Liturgy—was completed in Ukraine in 1878, and it went on to play an important role in the history of Russian sacred music. The legislation then in force in Russia forbade the singing and writing of church music unless it was approved by the Imperial Chapel. Tchaikovsky's Liturgy was published by Jurgenson in spite of the law, and the director of the Chapel, Nikolai Bakhmetev, protested against it. The matter ended up in court, and in 1880 Jurgenson finally won the battle, thus opening the floodgates for new sacred compositions.

Tchaikovsky completed a setting of the All-night Vigil in 1881. His *Nine Sacred Pieces* followed in 1885, after the composer promised to the Emperor Alexander III during their meeting in 1884 that he would continue to write sacred music. Setting a text from Psalm 141, '**Let My Prayer Arise**' is the eighth work in the latter cycle. It is one of the highlights of the Liturgy of the Presanctified Gifts, which is celebrated during the weekdays of Great Lent and is sung after the priest's exclamation 'The Light of Christ illumines all!' It is usually performed by three singers in the middle of the church in front of the Royal Doors. During the singing the congregation are on their knees as a sign of their realization of their unworthiness before God.

Artem Vedel (1767–1808) was born in Kiev, where his father worked as a wood carver. He studied at the Kiev Theological Academy, and was renowned for his fine tenor voice. He began conducting choirs in Kiev, and was later invited to Moscow to direct the choir of Governor-General Eropkin; he also studied composition with Giuseppe Sarti. After Eropkin's death, Vedel returned to Kiev to conduct the military choir of General Levanidov and, through his musical service, obtained the army rank of Captain. He spent his last years in an asylum.

Together with Maxim Berezovsky and Dmitry Bortniansky, Vedel is recognized as one of the big three composers of the Russian Empire at the end of the eighteenth century. He wrote twenty-nine sacred choral concertos in the style of the fashionable Italian opera so popular with the Russian–Ukranian elite, as well as ten concertos for four voices. While his works are sometimes criticized for being too sentimental, too operatic, and therefore non-spiritual, a number are still performed in Russian churches. His manuscripts, many of which are still to be explored, are kept in the library of the Kiev Theological Academy.

Vedel's '**Blessed is the Man**' is strategically placed in this collection immediately after Pavel Chesnokov's setting of the same text (from the All-night Vigil), which is based on a traditional chant, allowing a comparison between the 'Italianized' compositions of the eighteenth century and the 'truly Russian' style of the New Direction.

Anton Viskov (b. 1965) was born in Moscow. His grandfather was a church singer, and under his influence Viskov developed a passion for sacred music. He went on to study composition with Georgy Sviridov at the Moscow Conservatoire, and has since composed over two hundred works, including both sacred and secular choral music. He is heavily involved in the organization of Russian music festivals and educational concert projects, is the author of numerous publications on Russian music, and is a keen researcher of Russian folklore. He works closely with the Blagovest Sacred Music Ensemble, the repertoire of which focuses on the works of the New Direction. Viskov's music is widely performed, including by the Moscow Synodal Choir.

Composed in 2003 for the Moscow chamber choir Resurrection, '**Rejoice, Nicholas, Great Miracle-Worker**' is a setting of the first kontakion from the Akathist to St Nicholas. An akathist is a genre of Orthodox hymnography that appeared in Byzantine practice some time before the sixth century (when the well-known Akathist to the Mother of God was written). Consisting of twelve parts, it is a service for the commemoration and glorification of God, or a saint, and should be performed with the choir and congregation standing as a sign of respect (as its Greek name implies: 'akathistos' translates as 'not seated'). The characteristic feature of an akathist hymn is the repetition of the word 'rejoice' (*raduysya*).

TATIANA SOLOVIOVA

APPENDIX I: MONODIC CHANTS

Ia: Blessed is the Man
(*Blazhen muzh*)

Greek chant

Bla - zhen___ muzh, al - li - lu - i - ya, i - zhe nye i - dye

na so - vyet___ nye - ches - ti - vïkh, i na pu - ti gryesh - nïkh nye

sta,__ i na sye - da - li - schi gu - bi - tye - lyey nye__ sye - dye.

Al - li - lu - i - ya. Ya - ko vyest' Go -

- spod'___ put' pra - vyed - nïkh, i put' nye - ches - ti - vïkh

po - gib - nyet. Al - li - lu - i - ya.

Ib: Cherubic Hymn
(*Kheruvimskaya pyesn'*)

'The Repentant Thief' chant

Ic: It is Truly Meet

(*Dostoyno yest'*)

Znamenny chant

Do - stoy - no yest', ya - ko vo - i - sti - nu, bla - zhi - ti Tya

Bo - go - ro - di - tsu, pri - sno - bla - zhen - nu - yu i prye - nye - po - roch - nu - yu,

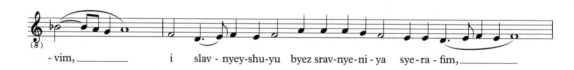

i Ma - tyer' Bo - ga na - she - go. Chest - nyey - shu - yu khe - ru -

- vim, i slav - nyey - shu - yu byez srav - nye - ni - ya sye - ra - fim,

byez is - tlye - ni - ya Bo - ga Slo - va rozhd - shu - yu, su - schu - yu Bo - go -

- ro - di - tsu, Tya vye - li - cha - yem, vye - li - cha - yem.

APPENDIX II: CYRILLIC TEXTS

Милость мира
Milost' mira
A Mercy of Peace

Милость мира. Жертву хваления.
И со духом твоим.
Имамы ко Господу.
Достойно и праведно есть покланятися
Отцу и Сыну и Святому Духу,
Троице Единосущней и Нераздельней.
Свят, Свят, Свят Господь Саваоф, исполнь Небо и земля славы Твоея;
Осанна в вышних, благословен Грядый во Имя Господне,
Осанна в вышних. Аминь.
Тебе поем. Тебе благословим, Тебе благодарим.
Господи, и молим Ти ся. Боже наш.

Благослови, душе моя, Господа
Blagoslovi, dushe moya, Gospoda
Bless the Lord, O My Soul

Благослови, душе моя, Господа.
Благословен еси, Господи.
Господи Боже мой, возвеличился еси зело
Благословен еси, Господи.
На горах станут воды.
Дивны дела Твои, Господи.
Посреде гор пройдут воды.
Вся премудростию сотворил еси
Слава Ти, Господи, сотворившему вся.
Слава Отцу и Сыну и Святому Духу,
и ныне и присно и во веки веков. Аминь.
Слава Ти, Господи, сотворившему вся.

Блажен муж
Blazhen muzh
Blessed is the Man

Блажен муж, иже не иде на совет нечестивых.
Аллилуй(и)я, Аллилуй(и)я, Аллилуй(и)я,
и на пути грешных не ста, и на седалищи губителей не седе. [Chesnokov only]
Яко весть Господь путь праведных, и путь нечестивых погибнет.
Работайте Господеви со страхом и радуйтеся Ему с трепетом.
Блажени вси надеющиися Нань.
Воскресни, Господи, спаси мя, Боже мой
Господне есть спасение, и на людех Твоих благословение Твое.

Слава Отцу и Сыну и Святому Духу
и ныне и присно и во веки веков. Аминь.
Аллилуй(и)я, Аллилуй(и)я, Аллилуй(и)я, Слава Тебе, Боже.

Херувимская песнь
Kheruvimskaya pyesn'
Cherubic Hymn

Иже херувимы тайно образующе
и животворящей Троице трисвятую песнь припевающе,
всякое ныне житейское отложим попечение.

Яко да Царя всех подъимем,
Ангельскими невидимо дориносима чинми.
Аллилуйия, аллилуйия, аллилуйия.

Не отвержи мене во время старости
Nye otvyerzhi menye vo vryemya starosti
Do Not Reject Me in My Old Age

Не отвержи мене во время старости,
внегда оскудевати крепости моей, не остави мене.
Яко реша врази мои мне,
и стрегущии душу мою совещаша вкупе, глаголюще:
Бог оставил есть его, пожените и имите его, яко несть избавляяй.
Боже мой, не удалися от мене,
Боже мой, в помощь мою вонми.
Да постыдятся и исчезнут
оклеветающии душу мою.

Свете тихий
Svyetye tikhiy
Gentle Light

Свете тихий святыя славы Безсмертнаго,
Отца Небеснаго, Святаго, Блаженнаго, Иисусе Христе!
Пришедше на запад солнца,
видевше свет вечерний,
поем Отца, Сына и Святаго Духа, Бога.
Достоин еси во вся времена
пет быти преподобными,
Сыне Божий, живот даяй;
темже мир Тя славит.

Гласом моим к Господу воззвах
Glasom moim ko Gospodu vozzvakh
I Cry Aloud With My Voice Unto the Lord

Гласом моим ко Господу воззвах
Гласом моим ко Господу помолихся
Пролию пред Ним моление мое,
Печаль мою пред Ним возвещу.
Призри, услыши мя, Господи Боже мой,
Просвети очи мои, да не когда усну в смерть
Вонми молению моему
Яко смирихся зело.

Достойно есть
Dostoyno yest'
It is Truly Meet

Достойно есть, яко воистинну блажити Тя, Богородицу,
присноблаженную и пренепорочную
и Матерь Бога нашего.
Честнейшую Херувим и славнейшую без сравнения Серафим,
без истления Бога Слова рождшую,
сущую Богородицу Тя величаем.

Да исправится молитва моя
Da ispravitsya molitva moya
Let My Prayer Arise

Да исправится молитва моя яко кадило пред тобою: воздеяние руку моею, жертва вечерняя.
Господи, воззвах к тебе, услыши мя: вонми гласу моления моего.
Положи, Господи, хранение устом моим и дверь ограждения о устнах моих.
Не уклони сердце мое в словеса лукавствия, непщевати вины о гресех.

Господи, спаси и Трисвятое
'Gospodi, spasi' i Trisvyatoye
'Lord, Save the Faithful' and Trisagion

Господи, спаси благочестивыя и услыши ны.
Святый Боже, Святый Крепкий, Святый Безсмертный, помилуй нас. [Трижды]
Слава Отцу и Сыну и Святому Духу, и ныне и присно и во веки веков. Аминь.
Святый Безсмертный, помилуй нас.
Святый Боже, Святый Крепкий, Святый Безсмертный, помилуй нас. [Трижды]

Многая лета
Mnogaya lyeta
Many Years

Многая лета.

Отче наш
Otche nash
Our Father

Отче наш, Иже еси на небесех,
да святится имя Твое,
да приидет Царствие Твое:
да будет воля Твоя,
яко на небеси и на земли.

Хлеб наш насущный даждь нам днесь;
и остави нам долги наша,
яко же и мы оставляем должником нашим;
и не введи нас во искушение,
но избави нас от лукаваго.
Яко Твое есть Царство, и сила, и слава во веки. Аминь. [Schnittke only]

Хвалите имя Господне
Khvalitye imya Gospodnye
Praise the Name of the Lord

Хвалите имя Господне,
Хвалите, раби Господа. Аллилуия.
Благословен Господь от Сиона,
живый во Иерусалиме. Аллилуия.
Исповедайтеся Господеви, яко благ,
яко в век милость Его. Аллилуия.
Исповедайтеся Богу Небесному,
яко в век милость Его. Аллилуия.

Из Акафиста Святителю Николаю
Iz Akafista Svyatityelyu Nikolayu
Rejoice, Nicholas, Great Miracle-Worker

Возбранный Чудотворче и изрядный угодниче Христов,
миру всему источаяй многоценное милости миро,
и неисчерпаемое чудес море,
восхваляю тя любовию, Святителю Николае:
ты же яко имеяй дерзновение ко Господу,
от всяких мя бед свободи, да зову ти:
Радуйся, Николае, великий Чудотворче.

Богородице Дево
Bogoroditse Dyevo
Rejoice, O Virgin Mother of God

Богородице Дево, радуйся,
Благодатная Марие, Господь с Тобою.
Благословенна Ты в женах
и благословен Плод чрева Твоего,
яко Спаса родила еси душ наших.

Любовь святая
Lyubov svyataya
Sacred Love

Ты любовь святая
От начала ты гонима,
Кровью политая
Ты любовь святая.

В молитвах неусыпающую Богородицу
V molitvakh nyeusïpayuschuyu Bogoroditsu
The Ever-Vigilant Mother of God

В молитвах неусыпающую Богородицу
и в представительствах мира непреложное упование.
Гроб и умерщвление не удержаста:
якоже бо Живота Матерь, к животу престави,
во утробу Вселивыйся приснодевственную.

Славословие великое
Slavosloviye vyelikoye
The Great Doxology

Слава в вышних Богу, и на земли мир,
в человецех благоволение.
Хвалим Тя, благословим Тя, кланяем Ти ся, славословим Тя,
Благодарим Тя, великия ради славы Твоея.
Господи Царю небесный, Боже Отче Вседержителю,
Господи, Сыне Единородный, Иисусе Христе, и Святый Душе.
Господи Боже, Агнче Божий, Сыне Отечь,
Вземляй грех мира, помилуй нас;
Вземляй грехи мира, приими молитву нашу;
Седяй одесную Отца, помилуй нас.
Яко Ты еси един Свят, Ты еси един Господь, Иисус Христос,
в славу Бога Отца. Аминь.
На всяк день благословлю Тя,
и восхвалю Имя Твое во веки, и в век века.

Сподоби, Господи, в день сей без греха сохранитися нам.

Благословен еси, Господи, Боже отец наших,

и хвально и прославлено Имя Твое во веки. Аминь.

Буди, Господи, милость Твоя на нас, якоже уповахом на Тя.

Благословен еси, Господи, научи мя оправданием Твоим. [Трижды]

Господи, прибежище был еси нам в род и род

Аз рех: Господи, помилуй мя,

исцели душу мою, яко согреших Тебе.

Господи, к Тебе прибегох, научи мя творити волю Твою,

Яко Ты еси Бог мой: яко у Тебе источник живота,

во свете Твоем узрим свет. Пробави милость Твою ведущим Тя.

Святый Боже, Святый Крепкий, Святый Безсмертный, помилуй нас [Трижды]

Слава Отцу, и Сыну и Святому Духу,

и ныне и присно и во веки веков. Аминь.

Святый Безсмертный, помилуй нас.

Святый Боже, Святый Крепкий, Святый Безсмертный, помилуй нас.